A NOTE ON
THE AUTHOR

Neil Ridley is an award-winning drinks writer and expert, a regular presenter on *Sunday Brunch* and contributor to the *Telegraph*, *The i*, *Wallpaper* and *Decanter*. He's the author/co-author of eight titles, including *Hot Sauce: A Fiery Guide to 101 of the World's Best Sauces*, which reached the top ten in the food book charts.

THE CRISP SOMMELIER

THE ULTIMATE GUIDE TO CRISP AND DRINK PAIRINGS

NEIL RIDLEY

Illustrations by
MALLORY HEYER

BLOOMSBURY PUBLISHING

BLOOMSBURY PUBLISHING
Bloomsbury Publishing Plc
50 Bedford Square, London, WC1B 3DP, UK
29 Earlsfort Terrace, Dublin 2, Ireland

BLOOMSBURY, BLOOMSBURY PUBLISHING and the Diana logo are trademarks of
Bloomsbury Publishing Plc

First published in Great Britain 2024

A catalogue record for this book is available from the British Library

ISBN: HB: 978-1-5266-7938-3; eBook: 978-1-5266-7953-6; ePDF: 978-1-5266-7952-9

2 4 6 8 10 9 7 5 3 1

Commissioning editor: Grace Paul
Project editors: Fabrice Wilmann and Athena Stacy
Typesetting and design: Chris O'Leary

Printed and bound in Great Britain by CPI Group (UK) Ltd, Croydon CR0 4YY

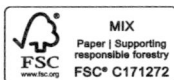

MIX
Paper | Supporting
responsible forestry
FSC
www.fsc.org   FSC® C171272

To find out more about our authors and books visit www.bloomsbury.com and sign up for
our newsletters

CONTENTS

ACKNOWLEDGEMENTS

A huge crispy thanks to the wonderful team of snack
fanatics at Bloomsbury Publishing – especially
Grace Paul, Athena Stacy, Fabrice Wilmann,
Cristiana Caserini, Isobel Turton and Shunayna
Vaghela – my fabulous agent, Martine Carter at
Sauce Management, Mallory Heyer for her wonderful
illustrations, Ted Dwane for his cider insights, Cadú
Gomes for his brewing prowess, Richard Osman for his
nostalgic inspiration, and to all the incredible snack
makers and drink artisans who have helped to shape
the deliciousness of writing this book. Finally, to my
family: Caroline, Lois and Honor for their suggestions
and for admirably acting as guinea pigs on several of
the weird and wacky pairings.

INTRODUCTION

To the snappy-dressed snackers, munchers, crunchers, nibblers, dippers and all you weird and wonderful crispy connoisseurs out there: have you ever wondered which crisp would work best with your Malbec, Martini or pint of mild?

If the answer is yes, then this is the book for you!

The Crisp Sommelier will give you a fun-yet-satisfyingly factual insight into arguably one of life's simplest but greatest of pleasures: the (un)holy matrimony of savoury-snack-based deliciousness and the cool, refreshing artistry of some of our favourite tipples.

If you're a little like me, then you'll know what I mean when I say I always feel slightly 'empty-handed' if I'm sitting there in a pub, bar or at home holding nothing more than a glass of wine, a pint, a glass of cola or a cocktail of some description. My other hand needs to be occupied, and this is where my fascination with snacks comes in. In recent years, I've become fanatical about exploring flavour beyond simply what's in the glass. Combined with the right snack, a drink can really, truly come alive in new and unexpected ways.

It could be that first refreshing sip of a pint of craft IPA, swiftly followed up by the welcoming rustle of a large bag of roast beef and mustard crisps, often ripped open to allow others to partake; what I've affectionately come to know as the 'English tapas' moment. It could also be the majestic discovery of how different wine-grape varieties have a symbiotic relationship with certain snacks, tantalising the palate to new heights. However, it could simply be the case that every great drink really needs a savoury companion to banter back and forth with.

Whatever your thinking is on the subject, you've come to the right place.

What you'll find over the coming pages is a smörgåsbord of suggestions of the best possible combos for drinks and crisps; the key aspects to look for in a pairing and creating the perfect harmony between flavour groups. Not only that, but we'll also take a cursory look at the history of the humble crisp and its hallowed position in society today: from cultural staple to gourmet essential. There's a chapter considering the current wave of fond nostalgia for some of our favourite brands from the past, as well as the ultimate dilemma: When is a Crisp Not a Crisp? Speaking of which, I've slipped in a few definite non-crisp interlopers, as I think the flow of the book is all the better for them.

On the drinks side of things, everything from beer, cocktails and mocktails, soft drinks to wine are covered and given a savoury partner in crime, with my thoughts on why they make perfect sense on the palate. You may be surprised by a few of them, or even mildly outraged by others, but that's really the point of the book: to inspire you to get matchmaking and discover your very own mouthfuls of heaven.

So, pour yourself something delicious and commence the customary rummage in that overstuffed snack cupboard – look, I know you have one, but there's no need to feel ashamed about it any more – this is all in the name of research!

Cheerio,
Neil x @Ridleydrinks

PART
I

A POTTED
(and Sliced)
HISTORY OF
THE CRISP

It's fair to say the humble crisp is anything other than humble.

In fact, it's at the epicentre of a flamin' hot, sizzling global infatuation – and some may say obsession – bigger than anything else in the canon of savoury snacks. In Britain especially, crisps represent such a significant part of the landscape of cuisine and food culture that it's hard to imagine life without them. But like all great ideas, they had to start somewhere, and some would say that was almost by happy accident.

> *Rather like the key ingredient – the potato – this story has well-established roots, and the origin of the potato crisp, or 'chip', travel deep into North American folklore. In particular, the kitchen of Moon's Lake House in Saratoga Springs, an upmarket town in New York State, famed for its horse racing.*

According to legend, in 1853 a wealthy steamship owner and socialite, Cornelius Vanderbilt, was patiently waiting for his evening meal, cooked by chef George Crum. The potatoes which arrived didn't impress the diner, who promptly sent them back for being too thick. What returned was a presumed act of revenge: Crum was said to have sliced them to an extreme thinness before baking them hard in oil. This defiance not only surprised and delighted their recipient but began a legend, and soon Moon's Lake House was famous across the country for serving its hallowed 'Saratoga Kettle Chips'.

While there's little provenance to back up the tale in its entirety, let's not let the truth get in the way of a good story. It is also, contrastingly, suggested that they were, in fact, invented by a different cook at Moon's Lake House, named Eliza, some four years earlier, and, completely conversely, by a British chef called William Kitchiner, in a recipe dating back to 1817. Whichever way you slice it, however, there's no denying that the touchpaper had been well and truly lit in the new world of savoury snacks.

Fast forward to 1910, and chips are big business in the USA, with Mikesell's of Ohio commercialising the cooking process and the likes of Lay's hitting the market in 1938 in the boot of creator Herman Lay's car. In London, a taste for the unmistakable crunch was also well under way, with Smith's launching the now iconic Salt 'n' Shake brand in the early 1920s, complete with its legendary paper slip of salt for consumers to season the crisps to their liking. By 1956, hungry Brits were munching their way through 10 million bags of them a week.

Other brands such as Dublin's Tayto, Edinburgh's Golden Wonder, Sunderland's Tudor, and Leicester's mighty Walkers – celebrating its seventy-seventh birthday in 2024 – were beginning to get in on the act, and fierce competition for new flavours began to grow, with cheese and onion fast becoming the nation's favourite, swiftly followed by salt and vinegar. Next came kitsch homages to the prawn cocktail and the roast chicken.

In tandem, by the late 1960s and early seventies, new types of crisps were being produced using corn starch, which puffed up when baked, first pioneered by Charles Elmer Doolin, the American-based inventor who created Cheetos in 1948. The likes of Quavers, Wotsits, Skips, Frazzles and Monster Munch (amusingly, originally called 'Prime Monster' in 1977) began to pioneer innovative, iconic shapes and more extreme flavour combinations, giving consumers a much greater choice and enjoyment factor.

Alongside these childhood staples, more independent, more upmarket brands started to grow, raising the gourmet angle to new heights, which not only focused on luxury flavours but the potato varieties themselves. In 1978, Kettle Chips was founded, later pushing the boundaries even further by launching competitions to find new weird-but-wonderful flavours, including Jalapeño Pepper and Spicy Thai. In 2002, the Tyrrells empire began, and the likes of Sea Salt & Black Pepper and Sea Salt & Cider Vinegar varieties helped enliven the palates of a more gourmet-led crisp connoisseur.

By this point, crisps had virtually entered a new higher form of appreciation in the snack world. Walkers helped to seal the crisp's future gourmet-led legacy by launching Sensations in 2002, with enticing flavours such as Balsamic Vinegar & Caramelised Onion and Thai Sweet Chilli still sitting at the top of the pile today.

And speaking of piles... I couldn't miss out everyone's favourite stackable snackable, the Pringle. First launched into the USA in 1968 (surprisingly, it would take a further two-and-a-half decades to reach the UK...), these tubes of joy not only represent how far the market has come, but arguably its future too. Astonishingly, you can buy a tube of Pringles in over 140 countries, with more than a hundred different flavour variants available. Serious food for thought there.

So, while the actual crisp may not be so humble any more, what is humbling is just how far it has come in a little over 120 years. I'll leave the final factoid to the creators of the rather marvellous Museum of Crisps (museumofcrisps.com) who have painstakingly catalogued no fewer than 1,344 separate flavours of crisps. Crikey. Just imagine the size of snack cupboard needed there...

Foie Gras, anyone? How about Evil Eye? Still no takers? OK, surely Cajun Squirrel, then?

TRUE OR FALSE?

1. *The Guinness World Record for the biggest collection of individual Pringles tubes is apparently 263. They clearly haven't seen my recycling bin after Christmas, then.*

2. *Walkers use 300,000 tons of British potatoes each year, the equivalent of 43,000 fully grown male African elephants.*

3. *It's been recorded that UK consumers munch their way through a ton of crisps every three minutes, enough to fill a phone box every forty-three seconds and an Olympic-sized pool every fourteen hours.*

4. *The inventor of the Pringles tube, Fredric J. Baur, died in 2008 and, as per his request, had his cremated ashes laid to rest in none other than... a Pringles tube. But which flavour, I wonder...*

Find answers on p.23.

TO CRISP, OR NOT TO CRISP?
Now that is the question

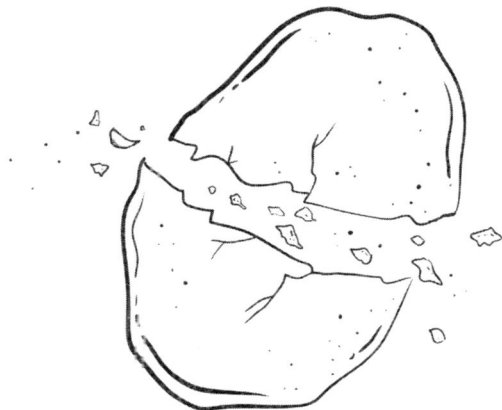

As existential scenarios go, this humdinger may perhaps be the proverbial $64,000, question and one can only imagine just how differently Shakespeare's famous soliloquy might have turned out had he been feverishly pondering what makes the cut in the fickle world of savoury-based snacks instead of Hamlet's seemingly trivial concerns over life and death.*

In all seriousness, though, this conundrum had been bugging me for some time, especially when it came to deciding where to draw the line on the pairings for the book. Should there be a definitive marker as to what actually constitutes a crisp and what doesn't?

- The consistency?
- The raw materials from whence it came?
- The cooking methods?
- The shape?
- The packaging?

While I'll freely admit that there are a few very definite non-crisps making an appearance in the pairings section, they are pretty obvious ones – and you'll clearly see I'm not just grasping at straws. However, in the interests of genuine snack professionalism, I thought it best to try and at least answer the above as best as I could.

In the broadest sense, the traditional potato crisp, or chip, is of course made from thinly sliced potatoes, which are fried in oil and then seasoned. However, when you start to throw in potato-related ingredients and other structural elements, the waters get a little muddier. Then, of course, you have corn-based snacks, such as Monster Munch, etc. To you and me, surely a crisp? In the eyes of the law, though? Well, let's test that theory.

While the international legalities and definitions remain vague and varied, there are some interesting examples out there that are worth nothing. For instance, in 1969, the US Food and Drug Administration (FDA) issued what's known as a Compliance Policy Guide or CPG, which was designed to safeguard the labelling of the words 'potato chips' on any packaging in America. What this meant was that only genuine slices of potato – fresh or dried – and nothing 'with significant amounts of added rice flour, corn

* Many a true word hath been spoken in jest…

starch, or other carbohydrates from sources other than potatoes, or which contain other ingredients not normally used in traditional potato chips' would pass muster.

In 1975, Pringles decided to challenge this in the US courtroom. Being that the construction – and texture – of a Pringle is clearly not just a curved, single piece of potato, it's obvious again that they contain other elements: in this case, corn, rice and wheat.

Incredibly, the courts decided that if Pringles were prepared to call out the potato element and content on the label, they could indeed be called potato chips. However, and this is where it gets a bit more confusing, they ended up calling them 'crisps'.

Now this is fine, of course, in Britain, where chips (as the Americans know them) are crisps. However, in the UK, everyone knows that chips are... well... chips... something you serve with fish.

The whole saga gets even more amusingly baffling in Britain, though, when it comes to which food products His Majesty's Revenue & Customs decides are VAT exempt or not. Under the regulations, 'potato crisps' are liable for a 20 per cent tax. In 2009, looking to gain a potential £100 million tax rebate, Pringles' parent company Proctor & Gamble decided to argue that Pringles weren't now in fact potato crisps but an alternative savoury snack.

After some lengthy debate, the initial argument that Pringles only contain 42 per cent potato was thrown out of court, but on appeal in the High Court, a judge overturned the decision, deeming the test of 'lack of potato-ness' sufficient.

So, like Mr Julius P, who adorns each tube, surely happy smiling faces for all those at Pringles? Well, not quite.

The case was escalated up the legal ladder again to the Court of Appeal by HMRC, and in a rather existential manner, the senior judge decided to discard the fundamentals of how much potato is needed to constitute a potato crisp and asked instead 'whether a reasonable man on the street would conclude that Pringles are similar to crisps and made from potato'.

He decided that the answer was most definitely a yes. Cue sad faces all round for Pringles.

Case closed.

Fast forward to 20 January 2024, and it seems as if history is repeating itself somewhat. Just like Pringles, Walkers decided to take a similarly opportunistic aim at the VAT regulations with its Sensations Poppadoms. The argument is like that of Pringles in as much that Walkers deemed its Poppadoms to be a non-VAT rated food item, rather than a crisp, with the following among the reasons: firstly, they're not made from whole potato, and they don't taste of potato. Secondly, they don't resemble crisps and they're designed to be part of a meal, rather than eaten as a solo snack, and, thirdly, because they're not called crisps or sold in servings like crisps.

Once again, it was a fairly one-sided verdict, in favour of HMRC – and it's hard to disagree, given just how easy it is to polish off a whole sharing bag of them on your own, just like it is the way with any of your favourite crisps. So, one could conclude that, despite what the law states, if you or I think a crisp is a crisp is a crisp, then it probably is. Ever heard the phrase 'if it looks like a duck and quacks like a duck, then it's probably a duck'?

A victory for democracy and common sense. Oh, and the tax man...

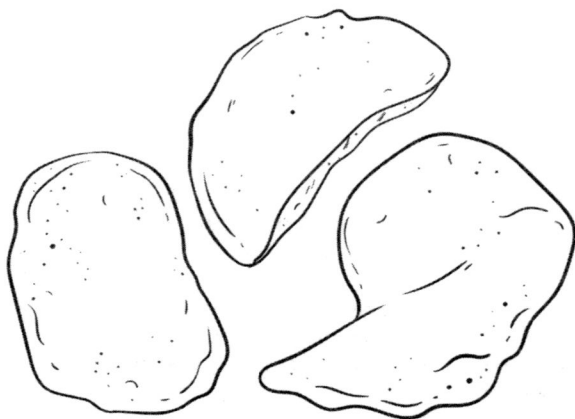

To Crisp, or Not to Crisp?

A TALE OF NOSTALGIA, AND... HEDGEHOGS?

Our fondness for crisp flavours of the past

As I was researching this book, I was hit by a wave of something unusually warming and comforting. However, I noticed that I was also feeling tinged with what can only be described as a slight melancholy. Then I read a tweet about when certain crisp brands first hit the shelves – from TV's favourite boffin and towering national treasure Richard Osman – which confirmed my biggest fears.

> *'1969: QUAVERS, 1970: WOTSITS, 1973: HULA HOOPS, 1974: SKIPS, 1975: FRAZZLES, 1977: MONSTER MUNCH, 1979: DISCOS... What a decade!'*

In barely nineteen words, the great man had not only summed up the unbridled giddiness of every childhood packed lunch I had enjoyed during the late seventies and eighties, but also, perhaps for the first time ever, made me feel like a relic of the past.

Nostalgia is a funny thing. At some point, rather like rheumatism, technophobia or bouts of flatulence, it will catch up with us all. Whether it's dusting off one's old Star Wars figures from the loft, drunkenly buying a Raleigh BMX Burner for a grossly inflated price on eBay, or simply surrounding one's self with packets of childhood snacks, nostalgia is a comfort blanket from the past, a reminder of youthful innocence, and a soothing voice that takes us away from the fears and strains of modern life as it gently whispers, 'It's all going to be OK'.

It's one of the reasons *Stranger Things* has been so stupendously successful and, in many ways, it's why the likes of Monster Munch, Frazzles and Wotsits have become such an important, unexpected part of our adult lives.

I say 'unexpected' for a reason. Let me ask you this: I'm willing to bet that if you're of a certain age, you had probably forgotten what a Pickled Onion Monster Munch tasted like, only to be instantly transported back to that moment you first greedily crammed handfuls of them into your mouth at school breaktime. As we become adults, we're supposed to leave things like this behind, broadening our palates with challenging flavours, choosing a dinner-party-sized bag of the likes of Walkers Sensations, or White Truffle & Barrel-Aged Feta Kettle Chips*, rather than a tiny packet of simple, uncomplicated, distinctly un-snazzy old Frazzles.

A lot of this newfound love for snacks of the past can be traced to their timelessness. Children today are really no different from the ones three or four decades ago, save for the smartphones and expensive sneakers. I rediscovered Skips and Hula Hoops because my own children wanted to try them and, quite frankly, I breathed a sigh of relief that they still taste as delicious today as they did all those years ago.

I'm a true believer that, like Greek gods, Knights of the Round Table, or Rylan Clark, the likes of Monster Munch, Frazzles, Discos, Skips and some of the lesser-known gems like Nik Naks, Space Raiders and Burton's Fish 'n' Chips will all become immortalised, their shining majesty casting a warming glow upon generations for millennia to come.

However, two questions remain. Firstly, which crisp flavours of the past expired before their time: unfairly consigned to the unforgiving Dustbin of Shame and secondly, which of today's crisps will be nostalgically enjoyed in years to come by the current Gen Z-ers and, now, Gen A?

Let's look at the second question first.

Again, dependent on your age or family status, you may or may not be familiar with Takis. The Mexican-made crisp in question has become a real hit, thanks to the brand's stupendously bold, spicy, chilli-laden flavours and distinctive rolled shape and colours. It's also a popular choice for online eating challenges, something my own teenage daughter has done with her schoolfriends, much to my amusement.

Not a real flavour, but if you work for Kettle Foods and are reading this, give me a call...

It's quite probable that, given a few decades, a wave of nostalgia will suddenly return to these now adults and, eager to demonstrate their resilience (or sheer foolishness), they'll once again take up the challenge, forgetting the, erm, 'consequences' of consuming too much chilli powder.

As to the question of which nostalgia-inducing crisp vanished too soon, for me it's an easy one. One could argue the case for the brilliantly titled Hedgehog Crisps, a now legendary fallen brand which began life in the early 1980s, developed by a pub landlord named Phillip Lewis. I remember gleefully being given a packet at our local pub, as my parents enjoyed the odd Babycham or three.

'They have bits of real hedgehog in them,' I remember proudly telling all my friends at the time, who were either equally impressed or quietly sick in the corner.

As it turned out, they didn't contain any hedgehog at all, a fact that wasn't missed by the Office of Fair Trading, which promptly closed the brand down for several years until they were relabelled as the apparently more acceptable 'Hedgehog Flavour Crisps'. However, Mr Lewis still got complaints from animal-rights activists (despite not one single hedgehog quill ever being harmed), and Hedgehog Flavour Crisps politely shuffled on until the early nineties, when they sadly disappeared into permanent hibernation.

Now if a flavour like Cajun Squirrel can make it in today's ruthlessly fickle snack world, I'm pretty sure that there's a place for the triumphant return of Hedgehog.

Until that glorious day comes, there'll always be a place in my heart for them.

THE BEAUTY OF CRISP
AND DRINKS PAIRINGS

Let's face it, most great things in life tend to come as a double act: Morecambe and Wise, Woody and Buzz Lightyear, Barbie and Ken, Claudia and Tess, Tom and Zendaya and now, Crisps and Drinks. The question is: why do they work so well together?

The simple answer points to the rise in a wider variety of flavours and descriptions of crisps, which are now more gourmet than ever, based on many of the tried-and-tested food partners you could expect to see in traditional fine food and wine pairings. Most crisp brands employ 'flavour maestros' to come up with incredibly accurate recreations of some of our favourite dishes, working in top secret lab-kitchens, where each recipe is a closely guarded secret.

Plain-old 'cheese-flavour' crisps simply won't cut it any more. Cave-aged, Wookey Hole Somerset Cheddar? Well, that's more like it! The bottom line, however, is that crisps offer a fabulously affordable option, if you're planning a more sociable gathering, to explore a night of perfect culinary partnerships. For only a few pounds you can cover off a wide spectrum of flavour styles very effectively indeed, without feeling the need to spend at least a month's rent down at the local artisanal farmer's market.

Then of course, there's the texture. Crisps offer distinct 'crispness' on the palate: an explosion of flavour in every crunch and a foundation on which to build your culinary vocabulary. They bring out inherent sweetness, savoury notes and top notes in drinks that weren't first apparent. It's no secret that most professional wine and spirits judges often reset the palate by munching on dry water biscuits or crackers between flights of drinks. The crisp really takes this to the next level by enlivening the tongue and the tastebuds, helping to prepare it for the drink you're about to enjoy.

HOW TO PAIR LIKE A PRO

I've put together a specific guide for you that explores some of the most significant flavour groups you'll encounter in crisps. You can use this as a handy reference to what to look for during the pairing process. The key priority is truly complementary flavours: elements where both the crisp and drink bring something different to the party, but when combined are greater than the sum of their parts and lead you to that incredible 'wow' moment!

WHERE AND WHAT...

First up: think about the occasion of the pairing: is this something for a weekend brunch, pre-dinner drinks, during a lively party or get-together, a sophisticated sit-down, or simply when you're chilling at home with a friend or loved one? Here you can elevate the style of pairing to fit any occasion: from the ideal type of wine or soft drink to the most appropriate cocktail. At the bottom of each pairing in Part II you'll find a little graphic that suggests which type of occasion the pairing will best suit:

Sophisticated Sipping

Couch Potato

Party Starter

Brunch No-Brainer

PAIRING DOS AND DON'TS...

The fundamental rule with pairing food and drink is that you want to avoid anything too dominant on either side: too powerful a flavour or style of crisp and you'll overwhelm the more subtle flavours in the drink and mask what's already there. This also applies the other way around: a bold Shiraz or smoky single-malt whisky needs a dance partner who is up for the challenge and won't just fold over flavourlessly at the first introduction. Another aspect here is still being able to identify where the flavours are coming from, so sometimes it's best to avoid pairing truly 'like-for-like' things, as you won't really be able to determine whether they come from the crisp... or the drink.

WHICH GOES FIRST? CRISP OR DRINK?

In writing this book, at least 150 different varieties of crisp were joyfully eaten, alongside the various drink categories in wine, beer, spirits, cocktails and non-alcoholic options. During the process I was left constantly thinking: am I pairing the drink to the crisp, or the crisp to the drink? I suppose this all depends on what you consider to be the most important partner, but here, for me, the drink probably takes the lead and is supported – and enhanced by – the crunchy delight of the crisp.

And so to the pairing process. What I found best was to take a small sip of the drink first: just enough to coat the palate and understand where some of its key flavours are coming from. Then as your mouth dries, take your first bite of the crisp. Note down the immediate headline flavours: how spicy/herbaceous/meaty/cheesy is it? What about the sweetness and saltiness? Did the combined flavours linger for long? Can you still taste the drink?

Then take a bigger sip this time and follow it immediately with the crisp. What are the differences? Has the partnership intensified and what are the complementary flavours? Has anything new shown up? Most importantly, is everything in harmonious balance? What about the texture too: has that added to the enjoyment in any way?

There are no hard-and-fast rules here: the key is to explore a few differently styled crisps with the drink you're hoping to pair it with. Sometimes the most obvious choices actually don't work at all and, conversely, something completely left-field works wonders!

ANSWERS TO TRUE OR FALSE QUESTIONS

1. *True*
2. *False (it's one hundred average-sized elephants)*
3. *True*
4. *True*

THE FLAVOUR DISC(O)

With the sheer multitude of different flavour pairings out there, crisp varieties and the flavoursome spectrum of wines, beers, spirits, cocktails and soft drinks, putting together an exhaustive list of descriptors would require a book you could barely lift, let alone dare place on a glass-topped coffee table or shelf.

So, what I've tried to do is create a universal flavour wheel or – drum roll, please – the Flavour Disc(o) (in homage to the legendary circular-shaped snack), which groups together what I feel are the most truly representative

ZESTY
VEGGIE
SWEET
SPICY
SMOKY
SALTY
ONIONY
NUTTY

OF DELIGHT

The flavour disc with segments labelled: CHEESY, CREAMY, EARTHY, FISHY, FRUITY, HEAT, HERBY, MALTY, MEATY

core elements of flavour. Hopefully you'll find this handy when categorising crisps' styles, but also when looking out for the explosion of wonderful flavours you'll experience in the pairings section. Some pairings will be very straightforward, with only a couple of flavours present: perfect and to the point, shall we say! Others will offer a much more comprehensive and complex balance of flavours.

Ultimately everyone's palate is different, but that makes this such a fun, exciting and personal journey.

PART
II

THE PAIRINGS

Over the next section, you'll find approximately 180 mouth-tingling crisp and drink pairings to explore and, hopefully, fall in love with. Along the way I've assembled combinations for the major grape varieties in both red and white wine, sparking wines, sweet and fortified wine, light and dark beers, ciders and then cocktails and non-alcoholic options. You'll find a couple of sneaky snack alternatives in there too, which were just too good not to include. You'll also notice that most of the crisps are from quite specific brands – but don't let that stop you: these pairings are designed to be universal, and you should get the same enjoyable results with any brand covering the same flavour style.

RED WINE

From bold, spicy palate sizzlers to sophisticated and complex fruitiness, red wine is utterly perfect to pair a wide variety of crisps with.

DRINKS GROUP:	**Red wine**
GRAPE VARIETY:	**Shiraz**
PERFECT PAIRING PARTNER:	**M&S Thai Chilli Rice Crackers**

Let's spice things up, shall we? As pairings go, the bolder the wine style, the more you're going to need something equally robust to sit alongside it as a perfect partner. Characteristically, Shiraz grapes (or Syrah to use their other name) – which hail from the Rhône Valley in France but are now hugely popular in Australia, New Zealand and the USA – tend to give a very full-bodied, tannic and complex-style wine, laden with underlying woody spice, dark fruits, tobacco notes and, in some cases, dark chocolate. Thai-style rice crackers, despite being small in size, are monumental in flavour, with sweet chilli flavours, a distinct malty note, a touch of liquorice and a hint of creaminess too.

Why This Pairing Works

The initial punch and crunch of the rice cracker sets the scene for an explosion of rich spice on the palate. As the wine develops, so does the intense spice, a touch of black pepper alongside a slightly creamy, unctuous, mouth-coating note, and a deliciously balanced fruity/sweet finish.

Flavour Groups

Heat/Sweet/Spicy/Earthy/Fruity/Creamy

Which Brands To Try

Penfolds Koonunga Hill (Australia), McGuigan Zero Alcohol-Free Shiraz (Australia), and Guigal Côtes-du-Rhône (France).

Red Wine

DRINKS GROUP:	**Red wine**
GRAPE VARIETY:	**Merlot**
PERFECT PAIRING PARTNER:	**Walkers or Lay's Roast Chicken/ Simply Roasted Duck & Hoisin Crisps**

An ideal dining partner when you're getting to know someone! Merlot is often derided as a particularly middle-of-the-road grape variety, thanks in part to its smooth, easy-going style and lighter fruity properties. In fact, its versatility makes it an ideal wine for pairing with food, and when you start to consider the potential pairings, the sky's the limit. Dependent on where it is from, Merlot can exhibit a range of flavours from lighter fresh cherries and plums through to more dense, slightly more tannic/tobacco and lighter spice notes, with vanilla and a sweeter meatiness, meaning it works well with chicken – especially noisin-style!

Why This Pairing Works

Because Merlot tends to be medium-bodied, more powerful flavours will dominate the palate. Roast-chicken crisps bring a slight sweet note, alongside a touch of fresh garden herbs and a lighter meatiness. Bring in the plumminess of the hoisin and you have a whole new thing going on...

Flavour Groups

Fruity/Herby/Sweet/Meaty

Which Brands To Try

Duckhorn Decoy 2019 (California), Oyster Bay Merlot (Australia), and Marques de Casa Concha Merlot (Chile).

DRINKS GROUP: Red wine

GRAPE VARIETY: Pinot noir

PERFECT PAIRING PARTNER: Torres Black Truffle/Tyrrells Truffle & Sea Salt Crisps

A pairing well worth foraging for, and no mistake. Pinot noir is undoubtedly one of the world's greatest grape varieties, favoured and revered by winemakers all over the world. Arguably the finest examples come from the Burgundy region in France, although other truly wonderful expressions can be found hailing from the Alsace region of France, as well as Germany, Chile and New Zealand.

Its fame comes from its unique balance of rich red fruits, light tannins, vanilla, black tea notes and a certain, highly unusual umami earthiness, often described as a mushroomy note or, in some extreme cases, forest floor. This last aspect is where our truffle-based snackage comes in particularly well indeed.

If you enjoyed this pairing, you may also like the pairing on page 66 (sherry/Torres Black Truffle Crisps combo).

Why This Pairing Works
On their own, truffle crisps can be something of a divisive flavour. When combined with the other charming aspects of a quality Pinot noir, they reach new highs, and the combo of the darker oaky notes and distinct umami flavours in the wine bring a savoury presence like no other.

Flavour Groups
Earthy/Herby/Fruity/Spicy

Which Brands To Try
Bourgogne Pinot Noir 2019, Domaine Philippe Livera (France), Berry Bros & Rudd Santa Barbara County Pinot Noir by Au Bon Climat 2020 (California) and Te Pa Signature Series Pinot Noir (New Zealand).

DRINKS GROUP:	**Red wine**
GRAPE VARIETY:	**Malbec**
PERFECT PAIRING PARTNER:	**McCoy's Flame-Grilled Steak Crisps**

A meaty masterpiece in the making! Malbec wines are famed for their robust, broad-shouldered heft, full-bodied smokiness and dark fruit notes, alongside meaty, almost gamey savoury flavours, and dried herbs. It is a hugely popular grape variety grown with extra-special success in the Mendoza region of Argentina (thanks to the perfect growing conditions), as well as other pockets of South America and California, although it originated in Southwest France and still has a small presence there. Malbec has become famed for being a wonderful companion to any roasted meat, especially certain cuts of steak, such as a sirloin, so it wasn't a hard choice to reach for a suitably big, broad-shouldered and meaty crisp like the classic (prime) rib cut of McCoy's Flame-Grilled Steak.

Why This Pairing Works

The bold, savoury saltiness and rich beefy notes of the McCoy's always take me back to Sunday roasts of old, no matter which day I'm munching on a bag. The sheer weight and tannic structure of a good Malbec brings out the meatiness further, alongside a touch of dark fruit, hints of tobacco and a dusting of spice.

Flavour Groups

Meaty/Spicy/Oniony/Earthy

Which Brands To Try

Terrazas de los Andes 2021 (Argentina), Casillero del Diablo Reserva Malbec (Chile) and Showdown 'The Bird' Malbec 2019 (California).

DRINKS GROUP: # Red wine

GRAPE VARIETY: ## Cabernet Sauvignon

PERFECT PAIRING PARTNER: ## Kettle Mature Cheddar & Red Onion Chips/Burts Mature Cheddar & Onion Crisps

The big one! Arguably the most significant red grape variety in the world, thanks to its incredible versatility and dynamic flavour profile. Cabernet Sauvignon began life as a cross between the Cabernet Franc and Sauvignon Blanc and is renowned for its well-structured, full-bodied bold flavours. It has it all: cherries, plums, vanilla, spices, leather and bold-but-balanced oaky notes. It's so popular that you'll find it in a huge variety of world wines and highly prestigious French wines (including claret), given that it blends so well with other grape types. Think of it as the foundations to a wonderful, expansive dream house; with each bottle, you try a different, beautifully decorated room. When it comes to pairing, the sky's the limit, but big, bold cheesy flavours are utterly divine.

Why This Pairing Works

A great Cabernet Sauvignon will mature well, its complexity developing as the years pass by. When paired with the deeper, more intense notes of a mature Cheddar crisp, you'll find a complementary palate of complex but delicious flavours. Arguably more of an after-dinner pairing than aperitif snack.

Flavour Groups

Earthy/Cheesy/Spicy/Fruity/Oniony

Which Brands To Try

Chateau Musar (Lebanon), Bread & Butter 'Winemaker's Selection' 2021 (California) and L'Epiphanie de Margaux 2020 (France).

DRINKS GROUP:	**Red wine**
GRAPE VARIETY:	**Grenache**
PERFECT PAIRING PARTNER:	**Walkers Sensations Regal Lamb & Mint/Kent Crisps Lamb & Rosemary**

Let's turn up the volume a little! Grenache, also known as Garnacha, is a wonderfully expressive grape variety which can trace its origins to the windy, arid climate of northern Spain, but can be found across the world now, and especially in the southern Rhône region of France, home to the popular Châteauneuf-du-Pape. Its charismatic style gives notes of fresh red berries (think strawberry and wild raspberries) alongside some sweeter, spicier notes of cinnamon, liquorice, aromatic herbs and fresh, sweet citrus. When pairing, consider these sweeter notes wisely: too much sweetness will be a little cloying on the palate and too little won't enhance the beautifully balanced fresh notes in the wine.

If you enjoyed this pairing, you may also like the pairing on page 45 (Sauvignon blanc/Lamb & Mint combo).

Why This Pairing Works

Lamb is one of the all-time great pairings with Châteauneuf-du-Pape, and the sweet, meaty aromatic note at work in both these sublime snacks is ideal. Here we have perfectly seasoned, slightly peppery meat, soft, sweet herbs, and a touch of saltiness to keep the bold fruitiness of the wine in check.

Flavour Groups

Meaty/Herby/Fruity/Sweet/Zesty/Salty

Which Brands To Try

Blason des Papes Châteauneuf-du-Pape (France), Chasing Rabbits Grenache (South Africa) and La Garnatxa Fosca 2020/21, Proyecto Garnachas (Spain).

DRINKS GROUP:	**Red wine**
GRAPE VARIETY:	**Zinfandel/Primativo**
PERFECT PAIRING PARTNER:	**Popchips Barbeque/Lay's Barbecue Crisps**

It's time to get grilling! Zinfandel, also known as Primativo, is a grape variety most associated with the sun-kissed Californian valleys (despite its origins lying in Croatia) and it will come as no surprise that it really wakes the palate up with its multi-layered jam-laden fruit notes and wafts of sweet, oaky smoke. As well as making a stonking red, it's also found as a ripe and fresh rosé variety. If ever there's a taste of the outdoors, with a touch of vanilla, ripe orchards and honeysuckle scent in the air, as the BBQ slowly comes up to temperature, it's this. So go bold, sweet, sticky and smoky with your pairing and you'll be beaming from ear to ear.

Why This Pairing Works

This pairing is all about dialling up the flavours, so you needn't worry too much about one thing overpowering the other. The medium-bodied style pairs beautifully to the sweet, hickory-spiced notes of the crisps and you'll soon be reaching for another glass... and packet.

Flavour Groups

Meaty/Sweet/Smoky/Spicy/Fruity

Which Brands To Try

3 Finger Jack Zinfandel 2019/20 (California), Carnivor Zinfandel (California) and Cero Zinfandel Alcohol-Free (California).

Red Wine

DRINKS GROUP: **Red wine**

GRAPE VARIETY: **Gamay**

PERFECT PAIRING PARTNER: **Torres Iberian Ham Crisps**

Gamay is not a name most red-wine drinkers will perhaps be familiar with at first, but this light-bodied, aromatic and floral grape variety will no doubt be more familiar in the French Beaujolais and Fleurie wines it has become synonymous with. Sharing its DNA with the Pinot noir grape, Gamay is a leading light in the slightly cooler wine-growing regions, including the Loire Valley in France and the Niagara Peninsula in Canada. Its softer but drier, more delicate fruit and lightly scented aromas and flavours need to be paired wisely to avoid total annihilation on the palate. However, get it right, and you'll find a gentle, sweet-singing gem, which can be enjoyed at lunchtime or the start of the evening.

If you enjoyed this pairing, you may also like the pairing on page 73 (Pilsner/Real Handcooked Ham & English Mustard Crisps).

Why This Pairing Works

Surprisingly, the slightly sweet and salty notes of charcuterie (especially Serrano ham) or roast chicken are a real hit with Beaujolais so much so that you'll be looking to take this pairing outside onto the terrace or to a picnic. The fruity notes sit wonderfully alongside the lighter saltiness and delicate meat notes, bringing out a lingering honeyed flavour on the palate.

Flavour Groups

Fruity/Meaty/Salty

Which Brands To Try

Louis Jadot Quincié Beaujolais (France), André Colonge Fleurie 2020 and Le Parfum 2023 (France).

DRINKS GROUP:	**Red wine**
GRAPE VARIETY:	**Tempranillo**
PERFECT PAIRING PARTNER:	**Pipers Kirkby Malham Chorizo Crisps**

Where the Grenache left off, Tempranillo picks up the flavoursome baton and runs off into the glimmering Spanish sunset! This hugely popular Spanish grape is the key component in Rioja and is the fourth most-planted variety in the world. Its versatility, easy-blending characteristics and ability to age well in oak mean that it comes to the fore in full-bodied, rich, spicy and dry, tannic wines, full of leather notes, tobacco and ripe fruit. It's no surprise, then, that some of the very best tapas meals I've ever enjoyed have often been accompanied by several glasses of Rioja, so think spicy, salty, fatty and bold in your pairing choice and you won't go wrong. Salud!

Why This Pairing Works

As an absolute staple in any tapas meal, chorizo brings some real sassiness and spice to the dinner table, with its biting saltiness and intense meaty spiciness. Any broad-shouldered Rioja should cope. The crunchiness adds another layer of intrigue and enjoyment too!

Flavour Groups

Spicy/Meaty/Salty/Earthy/Fruity

Which Brands To Try

Muga Reserva Rioja 2019 (Spain), Viña Albali SIN Cabernet Low-Alcohol Tempranillo (Spain) and Faustino VI Tempranillo (Spain).

DRINKS GROUP:	**Red wine**
GRAPE VARIETY:	**Sangiovese**
PERFECT PAIRING PARTNER:	**Torres Mediterranean Herb Crisps/ParmCrisps Original Parmesan**

The Italian stallion. Sangiovese is one of the most successful Italian grape varieties and is successfully grown right across Italy, with Tuscany being a particular hotspot. It has been described as a real workhorse from a blending perspective, and is one of the key components in Chianti and Montepulciano (an Italian grape variety in its own right). With flavours ranging from ripe strawberries, figs, aromatic thyme and hints of roasted vegetables, especially peppers and tomatoes, a bold savoury snack which holds its own in these departments is going to be a wonderful pairing, helping to really bring out the alfresco vibes.

Why This Pairing Works

The Italian herb notes match beautifully, with a lovely aromatic waft mixing nicely with the softer, red-berry fruit of the wine. Similarly, the slightly salty sourness and supreme punch of a toasted Parmesan crisp brings a touch of real Italian passion. Serve this as an aperitif before meals to really get your tastebuds in the mood. Bellissimo'

Flavour Groups

Herby/Cheesy/Fruity/Salty

Which Brands To Try

Ruffino Riserva Ducale Chianti Classico 2020 (Tuscany), Piccini Chianti DOCG 2022 and Montepulciano d'Abruzzo Riserva Tor del Colle 2019 (Italy).

WHITE WINE

From luscious, unctuous and full-bodied to crisp, fragrant, zesty and fresh, white wine makes for a wonderful partner for pairing crisps with.

DRINKS GROUP:	**White wine**
GRAPE VARIETY:	**Riesling**
PERFECT PAIRING PARTNER:	**Native Sweet Chilli Pr*wn Crackers/Walkers Sensations Thai Sweet Chilli Crisps**

One of the big hitters when it comes to white wines, the Riesling grape hails from Germany's Rhine Valley (but is also grown in Australia and the USA). It is a famously aromatic and expressive variety, full of tropical fruit and fresh floral notes. The wines are incredibly vibrant, with a touch of acidity on the palate balanced by sweetness. A deliciously chilled glass of Riesling is a great way to open the palate up as the starter to a more expansive meal, and it's a very versatile wine to work with indeed, meaning that Rieslings pair well with fresh shellfish, as well as creamy cheeses and even lighter Asian-style herbs and spices.

If you enjoyed this pairing, you may also like the pairing on page 57 (Prosecco/Tyrrells Sweet Chilli & Red Pepper).

Why This Pairing Works

The vegan 'Pr*wn' crackers have a touch of spicy sweetness which works superbly with the naturally sweet, aromatic notes of the wine. With some herbs – and a little heat too – you'll enjoy an explosion of sweet and sour flavours coming together alongside a creamy finish. A very moreish experience indeed.

Flavour Groups

Fishy/Spicy/Herby/Fruity/Zesty

Which Brands To Try

Jim Barry 'The Lodge Hill' Riesling 2021/22, Clare Valley (Australia), Ancient Lakes 'Eight Thousand Lakes' Riesling 2019 (USA) and Peter & Ulrich Griebeler Dry Riesling 2021/22, Mosel (Germany).

DRINKS GROUP:	**White wine**
GRAPE VARIETY:	**Pinot gris**
PERFECT PAIRING PARTNER:	**Tyrrells Vegetable Crisps/Kettle Lightly Salted Veg Chips/Eat Real Tomato & Basil Hummus Chips**

A sibling to the majestic Pinot noir grape, this white variety has a slightly pinkish hue to the skins and produces a wine that ranges from wonderfully spicy and bold to crisp and refreshing, dependent on where it is made. It's a popular variety in the Alsace regions of France and in Italy, where you'll find some of the very best Pinot grigio wines. Expect to find a lot of crisp, zesty zing with this style of wine, alongside a hint of softer vegetal notes and a touch of green orchard fruit. Another Mediterranean summer hit and a wonderful wine to pair with a lighter-flavoured crisp.

Why This Pairing Works

Think citrus, herbs and sweetness. The wine has enough freshness to cut through most things, but anything too dominant will linger on the palate. These vegetable chips have a natural sweetness, with a touch of garden herbs in the mix too, which really bring out the best in the pairing.

Flavour Groups

Zesty/Veggie/Herby/Salty

Which Brands To Try

Alluria Organic Pinot Grigio 2021/22, (Sicily), The Ned Pinot Grigio 2022/23 (Australia) and Tread Softly Everything Except (non-alcoholic) Pinot Grigio (Australia).

DRINKS GROUP:	**White wine**
GRAPE VARIETY:	**Chardonnay**
PERFECT PAIRING PARTNER:	**Brets Pesto Mozzarella/Tyrrells Pesto & Parmesan/M&S Honey Roast Ham Crisps**

Despite its world domination, Chardonnay remains a divisive grape variety and wine style, with some drinkers finding the creamy oakiness too dominant on the palate. I, however, absolutely adore its rich, buttery and almost creamy texture, working alongside the softer orchard fruits and ripe oily citrus zest. Some of the very best Chardonnay comes from the Burgundy region, with the likes of Chablis, Montrachet, Macon and Meursault attracting the most prestigious price tags. Fortunately, there are some excellent, more affordable examples of other wonderful Chardonnay from right across the world, including California and Australia among the very best. When pairing, think big, but not too bold, or you will lose the wonderful delicacy of a great Chardonnay.

Why This Pairing Works

The creaminess of the cheese and the rich herbaceous notes of the pesto really bring out the more fruity/oaky notes of the wine without dominating too wildly. Similarly, any honey-roasted ham crisp – avoid the mustard ones – tend to work, as the ham notes are sweet and smoky, which pair well with a more oaky-style Chardonnay.

Flavour Groups

Cheesy/Meaty/Creamy/Herby/Zesty

Which Brands To Try

Berry Bros & Rudd White Burgundy 2021 (France), Pure Vision Zero Non-Alcoholic Chardonnay (Australia) and Oyster Bay Chardonnay (New Zealand).

DRINKS GROUP:	**White wine**
GRAPE VARIETY:	**Sauvignon blanc**
PERFECT PAIRING PARTNER:	**Walkers Sensations Roast Chicken & Thyme or Regal Lamb & Mint/ Seabrook Lamb & Mint Crisps**

Sauvignon blanc is the very definition of dry and refreshing, with a wonderfully light, crisp mouthfeel and balance. The grape's heartland is across the Loire Valley in France, and you'll find it cropping up in some of your favourite Bordeaux whites too, such as Sancerre, where it brings a vibrant grassy freshness and drier mineral notes, alongside zesty flavours and plenty of tart green fruity notes. Sauvignon blanc is planted in South Africa, California and Chile too, making it one of the most popular New World wines. It's also broad-shouldered enough to pair well with grilled meats and herbs.

Why This Pairing Works

Both the Walkers Sensations are well balanced and not too dominant in herbaceous flavour, allowing the natural freshness of the wine to stimulate the tastebuds. The slight herbaceous note really works well with the citrus notes and the lighter meatiness brings a lovely aftertaste to the whole pairing.

Flavour Groups

Zesty/Meaty/Herby/Creamy

Which Brands To Try

Brancott Estate Sauvignon Blanc (New Zealand), Villa Maria Sauvignon Blanc (New Zealand) and Ara Zero Non-Alcoholic Sauvignon Blanc (Australia).

DRINKS GROUP:	**White wine**
GRAPE VARIETY:	**Picpoul**
PERFECT PAIRING PARTNER:	**Kent Crisps Oyster & Vinegar**

I remember about ten years ago coming across the name Picpoul with a wine-writer friend of mine over dinner and being truly thankful for her recommendation. Over the decade, it has become one of the most popular styles of wine, especially in the UK, thanks to its vibrant, fresh and very approachable palate, full of green, fragrant fruit (especially lime) and a deliciously crisp, slightly acidic floral note. The grape is predominantly grown around the Languedoc region of France in Picpoul de Pinet, which gives it lots of Mediterranean vibrancy. It shares a lot of flavour characteristics with Sauvignon blanc, so think bright, fresh flavours of seafood, well-seasoned green salads and lighter herbs.

Why This Pairing Works

The slightly saline, coastal flavour with the acidic vinegar and creamy potato are a match made in heaven with the lighter, fragrant-but-crisp fresher style of the wine. Both really bring out a lingering elegance but long-lasting finish.

Flavour Groups

Fishy/Salty/Malty/Zesty

Which Brands To Try

La Baume 'Cuvée Florence' Piquepoul Sauvignon Blanc 2021/22 (France) and Adnams Picpoul de Pinet (France).

DRINKS GROUP:	**White wine**
GRAPE VARIETY:	**Albariño/Alvarinho**
PERFECT PAIRING PARTNER:	**Chipsticks Salt 'n' Vinegar Discos/ pickled onion crisps**

If you've ever visited the Algarve in Portugal or Northwest Spain's Galicia and enjoyed the spectacular coastal dining on offer, then you'll probably be familiar with Vinho Verde: a bright, very young, fresh, almost effervescent-style white wine, which is served by the bucketload in the local fish restaurants and taverns. At its heart is the Albariño (or Alvarinho) grape, which brings a unique, almost unripe green-fruit taste to the wine and bags of sharp, citrus acidity. It's a great pairing with oily grilled seafood (especially sardines and calamari) and fresh green salads. It's also a real joy to pair crisps with, especially those that dial up the salty, dynamic flavours.

If you enjoyed this pairing, you may also like the pairing on page 97 (Gibson/Monster Munch combo).

Why This Pairing Works

A bold salt and vinegar crisp will bring you plenty of happiness in this pairing, with the coastal salinity bringing out the citrus/lime notes in the wine. For the ultimate pairing, though, combine the tart notes of pickled onion, which works well with the slight youthful, spritzy style of the wine.

Flavour Groups

Salty/Malty/Zesty/Oniony

Which Brands To Try

Wind and Waves Alvarinho 2022, Vinho Verde (Portugal), Chin Chin Vinho Verde (Portugal) and De Haan Altés Selection Diluvio Albariño 2022 (Spain).

DRINKS GROUP:	**White wine**
GRAPE VARIETY:	**Moscato/Muscat**
PERFECT PAIRING PARTNER:	**Lay's Cheese Flavoured Crisps/ Pringles Sour Cream & Onion**

A sweeter and altogether different experience. Moscato is made from the Muscat grape variety, which offers a broad palate of different styles of wine: from still white to red, and also sparkling/rosé. They all share similar aromas and flavours, which lean heavily on the aromatic side of things: think fresh, soft, fleshy orchard fruit like peaches, lemon zest and more perfumed notes like Earl Grey tea. Because the flavours are delicate, any pairing needs to be subtle and complimentary, so avoiding spices and anything too bold is important. Something particularly crisp and snappy will work very well on the palate, though, and a popular pairing has historically been soft cheeses. Make sure the wine's served super-cold though!

If you enjoyed this pairing, you may also like the pairing on page 63 (Tokaji/Bret Blue Cheese & Pancetta Crisps).

Why This Pairing Works

The cheese notes aren't too dominant and work well with the lighter, sweeter and fragrant notes in the Moscato. Similarly, the sour cream and onion is a classic crisp pairing in its own right, and is only heightened by this deliciously moreish combo.

Flavour Groups

Fruity/Cheesy/Herby/Sweet/Zesty

Which Brands To Try

Barefoot Moscato (California, USA), Gallo Vineyards Moscato (California, USA) La Spinetta Biancospino Moscato 2023 (Italy).

DRINKS GROUP:	**White wine**
GRAPE VARIETY:	**Gewürztraminer**
PERFECT PAIRING PARTNER:	**Walkers Sensations Lime & Coriander Chutney Poppadoms / Simply Roasted Duck & Hoisin Crisps**

A grape variety which sounds German but finds its roots in the Alsace region of France, Gewürztraminer is a sweeter-style, unusually aromatic grape which makes a deliciously rich and unctuous white wine. I say unusually aromatic because there's a signature waft of the lychee fruit in a classic Gewürztraminer and this gives you an idea as to the potential pairing style: think Asian cuisine and fresh-but-subtle spices. Gewürztraminer also grows really nicely across Eastern Europe and now in some top-class New World locations too, including Argentina, New Zealand and Israel. Like Moscato, it's worth keeping this as chilled as possible, which also heightens the senses for the pairing.

If you enjoyed this pairing, you may also like the pairing on page 68 (white port/Tyrrells Pesto & Parmesan Crisps).

Why This Pairing Works
From a textural perspective the miniature poppadoms taste superb with an ice-cold glass of Gewürztraminer. The bold flavours of the coriander lift through the sweetness and heighten the citrus aspects. Same goes for the Duck & Hoisin: there's a wonderfully spicy element that lingers on the palate, alongside a delicious fruitiness. Superb!

Flavour Groups
Spicy/Sweet/Heat/Fruity/Zesty

Which Brands To Try
Sainsbury's Taste the Difference Gewürztraminer (France), Colterenzio Gewürztraminer 2020 (Italy) and Pierre Brecht Gewürztraminer 2021 (France).

DRINKS GROUP:	**White wine**
GRAPE VARIETY:	**Viognier**
PERFECT PAIRING PARTNER:	**McCoy's Thai Sweet Chicken Crisps/Nik Naks Rib 'n' Saucy/ Herr's Baby Back Ribs Chips**

A grape that lives in France but has a holiday home in California! This classic, full-bodied white is grown predominantly in the French Rhône region but has found huge success in the warmer climate of the West Coast of the USA. Famed for its bold, punchy fruitiness — with ripe apricots, peaches, tangerine, honeysuckle and jasmine aromas — despite being drier in style. Its robustness will allow some fun experimentation with crisp pairings: think spices such as ginger and cinnamon, as well as spicy roasted meats working nicely with the other heady aromas in the glass.

Why This Pairing Works

The bold spiciness of the McCoy's is a surprising delight with the strong orchard-fruit notes and fragrant wafts of honeysuckle and jasmine. The slightly drier note of the wine also really helps to cut through the sweet, sticky note of the rib-flavoured crisps. A surprising discovery!

Flavour Groups

Spicy/Fruity/Zesty/Herby

Which Brands To Try

Majestic Nettie Viognier 2019, (California, USA), Sainsbury's Taste the Difference Viognier (France) and Babylon's Peak Viognier 2022 (South Africa).

DRINKS GROUP:	**White wine**
GRAPE VARIETY:	**Chenin blanc**
PERFECT PAIRING PARTNER:	**Jacob's Cracker Crisps Sour Cream & Chive**

Another Loire classic, but this time its leafy goodness has been transferred to the considerable winemaking talents of South Africa, now the biggest growers and producers of Chenin blanc in the world. Its light style has been harnessed in wines ranging from crisp and fresh to vibrant and sparkling, and it also ages well in oak for additional creaminess and spice. You'll find lots of green apple and pear in its signature profile, with honeyed notes and maybe a touch of lighter tropical fruit, so any pairing must be done carefully to avoid overwhelming the lovely delicate notes that great bottles of Chenin blanc bring.

Why This Pairing Works

Relatively lightly seasoned, the sour cream notes in these 'crisps' (OK, technically this is a cracker, but hopefully you'll agree on its addition) help to heighten the lighter fruit notes and bring a nice savoury crunch on the palate, while the chive works surprisingly well too!

Flavour Groups

Creamy/Fruity/Oniony

Which Brands To Try

Kumala Chenin Blanc (South Africa), Kleine Zalze Chenin Blanc (South Africa) and Honey Drop Chenin Blanc 2022 (South Africa).

DRINKS GROUP:	**Rosé wine**
GRAPE VARIETY:	**Grenache, Syrah, Sangiovese, Pinot noir, Mourvèdre and more…**
PERFECT PAIRING PARTNER:	**Burts Firecracker Lobster Crisps/ Proper Prawn Cocktail Chips/ Salty Dog Barbecue Rib Crisps**

As you'll also see on page 61, which covers sparkling rosé wines, the pairing opportunities are many for this on-trend wine. In fact, long gone are the days when rosé was seen as a naff option for someone who didn't really like wine that much. Today, rosé has become a highly revered category with some serious winemaking and grape varieties coming together as exquisite blends or single varietals, laden with fruit and perfumed aromas. Some are drier in style, with a delicate touch of floral charisma, while others err on the sweeter, more unctuous style. The key is to play to the wine's strengths: cooked shellfish, such as prawns and lobster work beautifully with a slightly sweeter rosé, and a bit of stickiness and spice, especially spare ribs, will pair with a drier-style wine.

If you enjoyed this pairing, you may also like the pairing on page 59 (sparkling rosé/Prawn Cocktail Skips).

Why This Pairing Works

Rosé wines are renowned for having a broader, more floral-scented and ripe-orchard-fruit profile, which partners gracefully with the sweetness and tomato notes of prawn cocktail crisps. Also dial up the heat a bit and the fruitiness really starts to come alive.

Flavour Groups

Fruity/Spicy/Fishy/Meaty/ Heat/Sweet

Which Brands To Try

Whispering Angel 2022 Rosé (France), McGuigan Zero Non-Alcoholic Rosé (Australia) and Bread & Butter Winemaker's Selection Rosé (California, USA).

DRINKS GROUP:	**Orange wine**
GRAPE VARIETY:	**Pinot grigio, Sauvignon vert, Albariño and others**
PERFECT PAIRING PARTNER:	**Tyrrells Vegetable Crisps**

Another distinctive shade in the technicolour palette of wine. Yes folks, orange wine is very much a thing, and it has nothing to do with the fruit at all. The distinctive colour (perhaps amber is a more graceful description) is created by leaving the skins of white-wine grapes in contact with the juice for longer before fermentation, which gives the resulting wine more colour and body. There's also a lot of biodiversity in making orange wine, with more organic methods often employed, and the wines can be distinctly funky in character, with notes of beeswax, honey, liquorice root and ripe orchard fruit. It pairs well with grilled meat and vegetables, so your crisp choices are far and wide!

Why This Pairing Works

The sweet, then savoury, earthy notes of the vegetable crisps play very nicely with the slightly funky, waxy note of the wine, helping to bring out a little more sweetness and fragrant fruit. The whole experience gives a really pleasing mouthfeel, the more root-vegetable notes helping to bring out some brighter, more fragrant notes in the wine.

Flavour Groups

Meaty/Salty/Earthy/Veggie/Fruity

Which Brands To Try

Tbilvino 'Qvevris' Rkatsiteli 2020/21 (Georgia), Bodegas Martin Codax Albariño Orange Wine (Spain) and Chapel Down Orange Bacchus (UK).

SPARKLING WINE

Sparkling wines are truly joyous for pairing crisps with. The effervescence on the palate really helps to bring the flavours to all the tastebuds, and this is where you can start to explore different textures too, especially crisps of the more puffed variety.

DRINKS GROUP:	**Sparkling wine**
TYPE:	**Champagne**
PERFECT PAIRING PARTNER:	**Walkers Classic Ready Salted/ McCoy's Ready Salted/Piper's Anglesey Sea Salt Crisps**

It's somewhat ironic that Champagne – arguably the most luxurious and most celebrated wine in the world, which has fuelled sporting triumphs, marriages, births and even a few 'dispatches' too, no doubt – is equally comfortable in the company of a packet of the most plainly flavoured crisps on the market. However, no matter which way you try to spice things up, the simplicity of this combination of humble flavours just... works. Champagne, which, by law, has come from the Champagne region of France, is usually a blend of grape varieties (Chardonnay, Pinot noir and Pinot Meunier), and the combination of creaminess alongside the yeasty and clean mineral notes can bring some wonderful flavours. Throw in a bit of age and you'll find more mushroom-like aromas too. Whatever you do though, keep the crisp simple. Et voilà!

If you enjoyed this pairing, you may also like the pairing on page 140 (sparkling water/salt and vinegar crisps).

Why This Pairing Works

There's something super-clean and elegant about a well-seasoned ready salted crisp. In fact, the seasoning shouldn't take away from the other two dynamics here: the texture of the crisp and the slight fattiness of the potato. This trio of perfection will bring out hidden depths in the Champagne: some oakiness, a touch of citrus zest and freshly baked bread. A simple masterpiece and one we should all enjoy. Champagne (and crisps) for everyone!

Flavour Groups

Malty/Salty/Zesty

Which Brands To Try

Taittinger Brut, Guy Méa L'Assemblage and Aldi Veuve Monsigny (all France). It's also worth seeking out France's other spectacular sparkling wine, Crémant, which can be produced widely across the country.

DRINKS GROUP:	**Sparkling wine**
TYPE:	**Prosecco**
PERFECT PAIRING PARTNER:	**Tyrrells Vegetable or Sweet Chilli & Red Pepper/M&S Prosciutto & Formaggio Crisps**

Whereas Champagne's beautifully balanced maltiness and zest needs little by way of flavour enhancement, a chilled glass of Italy's finest can really benefit from a little stimulation. Produced in the northernmost part of the country, in the Veneto and Friuli Venezia-Giulia regions, Prosecco's underlying flavour profile tends to be one of lighter, green orchard fruits with a touch of citrus zest and gentle honeyed sweetness. Here you can really have some fun and dig into more vegetal flavours – especially root-vegetable notes, including parsnip and beetroot, which work surprisingly well. Think about anything with a little hint of lighter, meaty saltiness too, such as Italian cured meats and roasted red peppers. There's one thing for sure: get it right and you'll experience *un momento paradisiaco!*

Why This Pairing Works

Differing from Champagne, Prosecco has a slightly lighter, sweeter, more fruity balance, which sits well with other flavours. The sweetness of the veg crisps are elevated by the bubbles on the palate, and the clean acidic balance of the Prosecco helps to cut through the slightly spicy, richer notes of the prosciutto, formaggio and sweet chilli.

Flavour Groups

Salty/Fruity/Zesty/Veggie/Spicy

Which Brands To Try

Della Vite Prosecco Superiore DOCG, Freixenet 0.0% Alcohol-Free Prosecco and Pale Fox Single Estate Prosecco Superiore DOCG (all Italy). Also seek out Ferrari Trento: not classified as a prosecco but another outstanding Italian sparkling wine.

DRINKS GROUP:	**Sparkling wine**
TYPE:	**Cava**
PERFECT PAIRING PARTNER:	**Ten Acre Fried Chicken/Real Hand Cooked Chicken Peri-Peri Crisps**

Hailing from the warmer climes of southern Spain, Cava has long been derided as a poor relation to Champagne – and of late, Prosecco. But write it off at your peril. This Spanish songbird sings with the voice of an angel when she's paired with the right foods. Cava tends to have a sweeter, more fruit-forward style than its other sparkly neighbours and when aged, especially for over eighteen months, it takes on much more refined, richer qualities. What's more, it's bottle-fermented like Champagne, giving it a more biscuity note than Prosecco – and a slightly more full-bodied profile means it can happily chat with even lightly spicy foods with the greatest of eloquence, so think big with your crisp pairings and prepare to be wowed.

Why This Pairing Works

The crisp fruit and acidity really cut through the unctuous, slightly spiced notes of the fried chicken and the citrus zestiness balances beautifully with the subtle-but-noticeable heat of the peri-peri, also helping to keep the saltiness well in check too.

Flavour Groups

Spicy/Meaty/Fruity/Malty/Zesty

Which Brands To Try

Gran Campo Viejo Cava Brut Reserva, Conde de Haro Brut Reserva Cava 2019 and Summum Lacrima Baccus Reserva Brut Cava 2018 (all Spain).

DRINKS GROUP:	**Sparkling wine**
TYPE:	**Rosé**
PERFECT PAIRING PARTNER:	**Prawn Cocktail Skips/Lister's Prawn Cocktail/Tatyo Prawn Cocktail Crisps**

Bearing in mind the huge range of sparkling rosé wines and the fact that some of my all-time favourite tipples are of this variety, this could almost be a separate chapter. One thing to bear in mind: whether it's a Champagne, Prosecco, Cava or New World sparkling rosé, the colour usually comes from what's known as skin contact (allowing darker-coloured grape skins to impart some of their vibrancy into the grape juice before it is fermented) or, in some cases, a blending of both white and red wines. Rosés are famed for their more perfumed aroma and sweeter, fruitier style, so pairing with lighter-flavoured shellfish – especially prawn cocktail crisps – is an absolute no-brainer. Time to think pink.

If you enjoyed this pairing, you may also like the pairing on page 52 (rosé/Burts Firecracker Lobster Crisps).

Why This Pairing Works

The sweet, tomato sauce-laden and faint coastal fishiness of a prawn cocktail crisp heightens the ripe freshness in the rosé, and the acidic notes and bubbles really make the lighter spices and peppery notes sing. What's more, the texture of a Skip just melts perfectly in the mouth with a few sips of a great rosé.

Flavour Groups

Fruity/Sweet/Fishy/Zesty

Which Brands To Try

Sainsbury's Crémant de Loire Rosé, Taste the Difference (France), Bosco del Merlo Prosecco Millesimato Rose Brut 2020 (Italy) and Chandon Sparkling Brut Rosé (Argentina). For a non-alcoholic alternative, try Kylie Minogue's Alcohol-Free Sparkling Rosé!

SWEET WINE

Traditionally these wines are the domain of the dessert, but with a little imagination they can work wonders with the right kind of savoury snacks, especially cheese-based, lighter style meats and, occasionally, a little heat and spice to cut through the sweetness.

DRINKS GROUP:	**Sweet wine**
TYPE:	**Sauternes**
PERFECT PAIRING PARTNER:	**Kettle Mature Cheddar & Red Onion Chips/Taste of Game Wild Duck/Wild Boar Crisps**

Traditionally paired with desserts or pâté, Sauternes is the crème-de-la-creme of sweet wines, famed for its wonderfully viscous, rich, full-bodied flavours, subtle perfume and ripe, zesty citrus fruit notes. The grapes (Sémillon, Sauvignon blanc and Muscadelle varieties) are left on the vines past the usual harvest time, where they develop what's wonderfully known as the noble rot: shriveling up and turning into sweet raisins. This process imparts a deep, rich, fruity note, and colour into the wine, with apricots and honey the predominant flavour notes. Because of the sugar content, it also ages well for long periods of time. When pairing a Sauternes, play to its strengths: think strong cheese, cured meats and some more spicy options for the flavour-adventurous.

Why This Pairing Works
With a wine this sweet, you're going to need something punchy to cut through and balance nicely on the palate. Strong cheeses (like Cheddar and Gruyère) will bring some nutty notes alongside a slight acidity and will highlight the softer fruit notes of the Sauternes. Similarly, any robust notes like game will bring a bold meatiness, which pairs wonderfully with the fresh citrus notes in the wine.

Flavour Groups
Sweet/Meaty/Nutty/Zesty/Fruity

Which Brands To Try
Tesco Finest Sauternes Château les Mingets 2014 Sauternes and Château Suduiraut (all France).

DRINKS GROUP:	**Sweet wine**
TYPE:	**Tokaji**
PERFECT PAIRING PARTNER:	**Bret Blue Cheese & Pancetta/Burts Smoked Crispy Bacon Crisps**

A Hungarian masterclass of flavour. Tokaji wines are highly sought-after in their domestic Hungary and neighbouring Slovakia, thanks to the range of unique flavours they possess, and are now very popular among wine connoisseurs all over the world. Tokaji is made in a similar way to Sauternes in that the grapes (chosen from six official varieties, including Furmint and Yellow Muscat) are left to develop *Botrytis cinerea* or 'noble rot', a type of fungus, on the vines, which gives the wine its charismatic sweet, rich, dried-fruit flavours when it is aged in casks for several years. Like its French counterpart, it pairs well with light and smoky meats, cheese, pâté and some spicy dishes, so will work well with anything strongly flavoured, especially blue cheese.

Why This Pairing Works

The rich intensity of the blue cheese notes are perfect partners for the sweet, zesty and fruitiness of the Tokaji, creating an explosion of complex flavours in the mouth. The smokiness of the bacon also brings out a honeyed note in the wine, which is delicious. Quite festive in many respects too... pigs-in-blankets crisps would be the ultimate!

Flavour Groups

Cheesy/Smoky/Sweet/Meaty/Fruity/Salty

Which Brands To Try

St Stephen's Crown Tokaji and Royal Tokaji 5 Puttonyos 2016 (both Hungary).

FORTIFIED WINE

Fortified wines such as sherries and ports are a real festive treat, often bringing some sweeter good cheer to holiday celebrations. There are also some glorious drier versions too, which pair wonderfully with salty, cheesy and drier aromatic snacks.

DRINKS GROUP:	**Fortified wine**
TYPE:	**Sherry – manzanilla, fino and oloroso**
PERFECT PAIRING PARTNER:	**Manomasa Manchego & Green Olive Tortilla Chips/Pipers Kirkby Malham Chorizo/Torres Black Truffle Crisps**

There's nothing quite like tapas: a fabulously convivial sharing experience where a little seems to go a long way. And if you're really going to properly explore this delectable dining delight, you need the subtle flavours of sherry in your hand. Dry sherries such as fino and manzanilla have a solid saline backbone, alongside some superb aromatic/herbaceous aromas and mouthwatering zesty qualities, which help to cut through the intense flavours of tapas dishes like chorizo cooked in red wine, manchego cheese and patatas bravas. Oloroso sherry brings a touch of aged nuttiness, as well as sweetness, which really suits more complex flavours like truffle and roasted peppers. Time to break out the flamenco music for your palate to start dancing!

If you enjoyed this pairing, you may also like the pairing on page 38 (Tempranillo/Pipers Kirkby Malham Chorizo Crisps).

Why This Pairing Works
The bone-dry sherry styles (especially when served with tonic over ice) just ooze charisma when paired with manchego crisps: salty notes intermingle with lemon zest and some more meaty notes develop. The sherry also slices through the fattiness in chorizo crisps, bringing sweetness too. Oloroso sherries have such a unique nutty character that they partner up with the slightly earthy qualities of truffle, and a touch of salt helps to bring out even more complexity.

Flavour Groups
Salty/Cheesy/Meaty/Spicy/Nutty

Which Brands To Try
Gonzalez Byass Tio Pepe Fino, La Gitana Manzanilla and Gonzalez Byass Alfonso Oloroso Seco Sherry (all Spain).

DRINKS GROUP: # Fortified wine

TYPE: ## Port – ruby and tawny

PERFECT PAIRING PARTNER: ## Kettle Mature Cheddar & Red Onion Chips/Simply Roasted Duck & Hoisin Crisps/Proper Barbecue Lentil Chips

Portugal's Porto is a city steeped in wine heritage. Legendary port houses line the banks of the River Douro, including Taylor's, Graham's, Niepoort, Sandeman and Quinta do Noval. It's a magical place to visit, especially for the cuisine. Red port is made from predominantly five grape varieties, which grow in the Douro Valley and give a rich, rounded fruitiness. The wine is fortified with a grape spirit and is then matured in vast tanks (ruby taking the name from its wonderful bright hues) or oak barrels (tawny, which has a sublime, nutty complexity). A festive staple paired with blue cheese, both styles are also wonderful with other food, including richly flavoured meat, pâtés and some lighter spicy dishes.

Why This Pairing Works

The incredibly rich fruitiness and sweetness is a no-brainer to pair with strong cheese, and the Cheddar & Red Onion provides a solid savoury backbone with every delicious mouthful. The Roasted Duck turns up the savoury notch a touch, with the port bringing more sticky complexity of dark chocolate and plum notes. Barbecue brings a touch of spice and nuttiness, working in harmony with a nicely aged tawny port.

Flavour Groups

Sweet/Spicy/Cheesy/Meaty/Nutty

Which Brands To Try

Graham's 2017 Late Bottled Vintage, Taylor's 20-Year-Old Tawny and Sandeman Fine Ruby Port (all Portugal).

DRINKS GROUP:	**Fortified wine**
TYPE:	**Port – white**
PERFECT PAIRING PARTNER:	**Tyrrells Pesto & Parmesan Crisps/Made For Drink Chorizo Thins/Serious Pig Crunchy Snacking Cheese**

White port – and its more uncommon counterpart, rosé – is, ironically, something of a dark horse in the world of fortified wines, having lived in the shadow of their two more famous siblings (ruby and tawny) for some time – until now. Made in a similar way, but from a different grape variety, white port can take on a sweet, fresh and floral flavour profile, or something a lot drier and not dissimilar to that of a fino sherry. Both styles are utterly irresistible when paired with tapas-style food: cured meats, manchego and goat's cheeses, as well as lighter shellfish.

Why This Pairing Works

Some curveballs here in the snack world: the Chorizo Thins are of course made from chorizo, but I think you'll agree they deserve their place here, thanks to the wonderful salty, meaty goodness, which works extremely well with a drier-style white port. If you're going for something sweeter, the Pesto & Parmesan Crisps really help to cut through the syrupiness and bring out more floral, fruity flavours.

Same goes for the Serious Pig snacks (again, something of a cheesy curveball!).

Flavour Groups

Fruity/Sweet/Salty/Cheesy

Which Brands To Try

Try mixing it with tonic and ice. Taylor's Chip Dry White Port, Cockburn's Fine White Port and Kopke 10-Year-Old White Port (all Portugal).

Fortified Wine

LIGHT BEER

*Beer of any kind –
be it lager, bitter,
stout or non-alcoholic
variants – is full of
malty flavour, which
pairs wonderfully
with crisps.*

DRINKS GROUP:	**Light beer**
TYPE:	**IPA**
PERFECT PAIRING PARTNER:	**Kent Crisps Oyster & Vinegar/ Burts Sea Salt & Malt Vinegar Crisps**

Happiness is hoppiness! The sheer range of flavours in a well-made India pale ale – or IPA – will put most other drinks to shame, and it's easy to see why the craft-beer movement has been largely propelled along by this pulsating, punchy pint for the last few decades or so. Historically, the pale ales of the eighteenth century were far less pungent, and hops have been used traditionally to give a beer its overriding bitterness. In more modern times, aromatic hop styles such as Citra, Cascade, Mosaic and Amarillo bring brighter intense top notes of citrus (grapefruit and lemon zest), pine and, in some cases, tropical fruit and spice. Any pairings need to be robust enough to handle these aromas and sharp bitterness, but also provide a bit of a cushion in the mouth.

Why This Pairing Works
The floral top notes and bitterness in the IPA are heightened by the initial sweet maltiness of the crisp before the saltiness really begins to work its magic. The citrus notes are enlivened, and the slight oiliness of the crisp keeps the sharp notes of the hops in check. The whole experience is vibrant, fresh and invites to you take sip and bite after sip and bite.

Flavour Groups
Malty/Zesty/Salty

Which Brands To Try
The Kernel India Pale Ale, Beavertown Lazer Crush Alcohol-Free IPA, Thornbridge Brewery Jaipur (all UK).

DRINKS GROUP:	**Light beer**
TYPE:	**Pilsner**
PERFECT PAIRING PARTNER:	**Real Handcooked Ham & English Mustard/Salty Dog Ham & Mustard/Two Farmers Hereford Hop Cheese & Onion Crisps**

Pilsner beers tend to be less hop-forward than IPAs, but nonetheless have a wonderfully aromatic crispness to them. The name originally hails from Plzeň in the Czech Republic, where the first, Pilsner Urquell, was brewed in the mid-nineteenth century. The flavour profile of this traditional Bohemian Pilsner tends to be slightly malty, with a lighter bitterness and moderate aromatic note, with German-style Pilsners a little lighter and more earthy on the palate. As such, they pair very well with traditional hard cheeses with plenty of character and bite, although lighter meats, such as ham, are also very much in the flavoursome ballpark too.

Why This Pairing Works

The lighter, slightly smoky-sweet notes of the ham are a total delight when combined with the well-balanced maltiness and crisp bitterness of a Pilsner, with the mustard helping to bring out more aromatic character. Similarly, the drier bite of a stronger cheese crisp will really tantalise the tongue and allow the maltiness to develop.

Flavour Groups

Malty/Meaty/Cheesy/Zesty

Which Brands To Try

Pilsner Urquell (Czech Republic), Krombacher Non-Alcoholic Pils (Germany) and Jupiler (Belgium) (plus an honourable mention to Br3wery, my local brewpub in Beckenham, Kent, for an excellent Pilsner).

DRINKS GROUP:	**Light beer**
TYPE:	**Wheat beer**
PERFECT PAIRING PARTNER:	**Walkers Wotsits Cheese/Walkers Quavers Cheese/crunchy banana chips**

Wheat beer has a characterful style, full of fruity, creamy notes and a distinctly ripe banana-led aroma and flavour (think banana bread) thanks to the style of fermentation and the significance of the wheat in the 'mash' (the start of fermentation, where crushed grains are added). Wheat beer – sometimes called white beer – is popular in Belgium, where brands like Hoegaarden are brewed with coriander and orange peel, a style that dates back to the fifteenth century, to give a complex citrusy, spicy note into the mix. Its distinct cloudiness comes from bottle conditioning: an additional fermentation once it has been bottled. Wheat beer isn't particularly bitter, and anything mildly cheesy or with a hint of subtle spice should work well with the lovely creamy and citrus notes.

Why This Pairing Works

The mildness of Wotsits and Quavers brings a subtlety to the pairing and doesn't overshadow the delicious fruit notes in the beer. One thing to consider here is the smooth, creamy mouthfeel a softer, puffed corn snack brings to the whole experience. As a wildcard, dial up those banana bread notes by pairing it with dried banana chips!

Flavour Groups

Creamy/Cheesy/Zesty/Malty

Which Brands To Try

Hoegaarden (Belgium), Blue Moon (USA) and Erdinger Alkoholfrei non-alcoholic (Germany).

DRINKS GROUP:	**Light beer**
TYPE:	**Lager**
PERFECT PAIRING PARTNER:	**Walkers Salt & Vinegar Crisps/ prawn crackers/Poppadoms Originals**

Arguably the most popular style of beer in the world and the one most likely to be paired with something crunchy and flavoursome. A rite of passage in any pub, so strong that they wrote songs about it (well, one, called 'Two Pints of Lager and a Packet of Crisps Please'). No matter which lager you choose, be it a classic Stella, Carling, Carlsberg, European (like Peroni) or something from further afield, like Asahi from Japan, India's Kingfisher, Cobra or a Chang from Thailand, your pairing isn't going to be ruined by the wrong crisp. Staple pub classics like Walkers, to prawn crackers and poppadoms will all serve admirably. Having said that, sharper salt and vinegar notes bring out the maltiness and dial up the thirst-quenching potential.

Why This Pairing Works

Lagers, especially domestic styles, are all about refreshment, so the saltiness and touch of tart vinegar will bring out the fresh crispness of any pint and add to its malty foundations. More varied lagers bring in sweet creaminess and soak up flavour – especially if they are brewed using rice, which gives a lighter flavour and a hint of crisp dryness on the finish.

There's nothing quite like a beautifully chilled Asian beer, a prawn cracker and a small bowl of sweet-chilli dipping sauce. Perfection!

Flavour Groups

Salty/Malty/Creamy/Zesty

Which Brands To Try

Estrella Damm (Spain), Kingfisher (India), Chang (Thailand) and Lucky Saint non-alcoholic (UK).

DRINKS GROUP:	**Light beer**
TYPE:	**Saison**
PERFECT PAIRING PARTNER:	**Walkers Roast Chicken/ Sensations Roast Chicken & Thyme Crisps**

Saison is a style of beer which has seen a resurgence of interest from craft brewers, thanks to its traditionally heavier fermentation and distinctly funkier flavours. The name comes from the French word for 'season' and, historically, these were beers made mostly out of necessity in Wallonian farmhouses in Belgium, from whatever grain crop was being harvested: be it wheat, barley or rye, for example. Saisons traditionally have a higher carbonation and a slightly spicier, almost peppery character, although the style has been explored all over the world, with each beer taking on different stylistic elements. Try to watch out for any crisp too rich in spice or garlic, which can really interfere with some of the lighter, beautiful fragrances in this beer.

If you enjoyed this pairing, you may also like the pairing on page 45 (Sauvignon blanc/Walkers Sensations Roast Chicken & Thyme Crisps).

Why This Pairing Works
The 'swavoury' (sweet 'n' savoury), lighter meatiness and herbaceous nature of a classic roast-chicken crisp is a match made in heaven for a classic effervescent Saison, the higher carbonation helping to bring out the peppery notes and some of the lovely fruity notes in the beer. Dependent on which one you choose, you may find a slight (most welcome) maltiness too.

Flavour Groups
Meaty/Malty/Fruity/Herby

Which Brands To Try
Saison Dupont (Belgium), Paljas Saison (Belgium) Insel-Brauerei Swimmers Saison (low alcohol) (Germany) and Thornbridge Mind Games Saison (UK).

DRINKS GROUP:	**Light beer**
TYPE:	**Blonde**
PERFECT PAIRING PARTNER:	**Walkers Max Punchy Paprika/ Tyrrells Smoked Paprika Crisps**

Despite the usually small stature and bottle size, this light beer has a highly characterful style. Rich notes of deep malt, a thread of fresh lemon zest, and heady aromatic spices can all be found in abundance, alongside their high-alcohol strength. Blonde beer doesn't tend to be particularly bitter – or refreshingly crisp – but offers huge complexity. As a result, sweeter spices, such as paprika, work very nicely indeed, offering an additionally bold and heady flavour.

Why This Pairing Works

The initial sweetness of the crisp really helps to build a foundation for the naturally sweeter, malty notes in the beer; then the sweet smokiness of the spices waft in, blending well with the citrus and coriander flavours. It's a bold pairing and not one for everyone due to its complexity, but something to sip and savour.

Flavour Groups

Malty/Spicy/Fruity/Zesty/Smoky

Which Brands To Try

Chimay Blonde, Leffe Blonde and Duvel Strong Blonde (all Belgium).

DRINKS GROUP:	**Light beer**
TYPE:	**Sour**
PERFECT PAIRING PARTNER:	**Torres Cured Cheese Crisps / Howdah Masala Dippers**

Sour beers are a relatively new addition to the taps of our favourite craft-brew pubs, and they certainly divide opinion with their distinctive – and intentionally acidic – flavour, thanks to the addition of wild yeasts into the fermentation process. The principle isn't new at all and has been a skilful technique used in Belgian lambic beers (see page 88) since the thirteenth century and in some German weisse beers. The strong sour flavour and additional fruit notes, such as peach, mango and lemon, make it tricky to pair. But pair we must, and the high carbonation and acidity helps it cut through bold, fatty flavours and salinity, so think big, meaty, spicy and cheesy!

Why This Pairing Works

With a non-fruity sour, you'll be looking for something which complements the bold acidic flavours but offers something else. Try a punchy, full-bodied cheesy crisp too, with the beer's acidity cutting through the fattiness and the fizz helping to clean the palate for the next mouthful. With something more fruit-driven, try a sweeter-style, more curry-inspired crisp, like the Masala Dippers, which have a slight tropical-fruit note to them.

Flavour Groups

Zesty/Earthy/Spicy/Cheesy/Fruity

Which Brands To Try

Signature Brew Lemon Citra, Orbit Beers Tzatziki Sour and Vault City Triple Fruited Mango (all UK).

DARK BEER

The rich, amber nuttiness in a dark beer is prime territory for crisp pairings with a bolder, meaty flavour.

DRINKS GROUP:	**Dark beer**
TYPE:	**Bitter ale**
PERFECT PAIRING PARTNER:	**Pipers Great Berwick Longhorn Beef/McCoy's Flame-Grilled Steak/Sussex Crisp Co. Rib of Sussex Beef with Horseradish Crisps**

In the pantheon of pairings, a pint of bitter and a packet of crisps might just be the very essence of perfection. Ale, particularly the British style, with its refined maltiness, nut-brown colour and sublime bitterness, is a joy to work with as a flavoursome canvas. Because most bitters aren't too high in strength or overly carbonated, the distinct notes of freshly baked bread, darker malt and rich, toasted sweetness lend themselves perfectly to roasted-meat flavours, where the caramelisation helps to bring out enormous complexity on the palate. It's why a pint of ale and a pub Sunday roast just sings exquisitely, and why you really can't go wrong or need to look further than a solid, dependable packet of roast-beef crisps.

Why This Pairing Works

The meatiness of the crisps, with the herbaceous and onion flavours, brings out a caramel note in the beer, and the saltiness helps to balance any sweeter notes on the palate. The whole experience is complex, rich and utterly delightful. A classic – hard to better, in my humble opinion!

Flavour Groups

Meaty/Oniony/Salty/Malty/Herby/Nutty

Which Brands To Try

London Pride, Old Speckled Hen and Innis & Gunn The Original Cask-Matured Ale (all UK).

Dark Beer

DRINKS GROUP:	**Dark beer**
TYPE:	**Stout and Porter**
PERFECT PAIRING PARTNER:	**Bacon fries/smoky bacon crisps**

In the canon of dark beer, stout arguably sits at the very top in terms of its legendary status, mostly thanks to the work of one Arthur Guinness in Dublin and his iconic brand. The distinctive taste and dark colour come from the use of roasted barley and malt extract, which gives the wondrous coffee, dark chocolate and richer dried-fruit notes, alongside the creamy texture. Stout, like its sibling, porter (which historically tended to be slightly lighter in colour and less full-bodied in flavour, unlike today, where both share many similarities), can be a divisive flavour, but the darker, almost smoky flavours and bitter backbone are best paired with sweeter, slightly smokier flavours, and one fits the bill perfectly: smoky bacon!

Why This Pairing Works

Smoky bacon crisps are surprisingly sweet, alongside the deliciously moreish wafts of woodsmoke, meaning they balance out the dry bitterness of the stout first and foremost, but then add other layers of subtle meatiness and smoke, which really suits the heavenly malty, dark-roasted coffee notes in the beer.

Flavour Groups

Smoky/Meaty/Malty/Earthy

Which Brands To Try

Guinness Export (or Guinness 0.0 non-alcoholic) (Ireland), Badger Master Stout (Scotland) and Black Sheep Milk Stout (England).

Dark Beer

DRINKS GROUP:	**Dark beer**
TYPE:	**Red ale**
PERFECT PAIRING PARTNER:	**Popchips Barbeque/Pringles Texas BBQ Sauce**

Ireland's contribution to global brewing history is hugely significant, and the distinct, dark flavours of stout can be found pretty much all over the world now. However, there's another, perhaps less-well-known tradition of red ale in the country, which is also as significant to the Irish brewing legacy. Brewers such as Smithwick's and Sullivan's of Kilkenny can trace their roots back to the early 1700s. Red ales have a distinctly nutty, almost caramel maltiness to them, with a buttery, spiced-toffee aroma and creamy, lightly bitter taste, which pairs very nicely with smoky-sweet barbecue flavours and grilled meat.

If you enjoyed this pairing, you may also like the pairing on page 36 (Zinfandel/Popchips Barbeque/Lay's Barbecue Crisps).

Why This Pairing Works
The sweet smoky notes of the barbecue really help the richly textured, caramelised maltiness of the ale to come alive, and combined, they deliver an intense, almost sizzling, palate-coating experience of bittersweet nuttiness, which is very moreish indeed. If you're not a stout fan, this is equally as complex, but less of a heavyweight combo than its other Irish counterpart.

Flavour Groups
Sweet/Nutty/Malty/Spicy/Meaty

Which Brands To Try
Smithwick's Irish Red Ale, Galway Bay Brewery Red Ale (Ireland) and St Peter's Ruby Red Ale (UK).

Dark Beer

DRINKS GROUP:	**Dark beer**
TYPE:	**Brown ale**
PERFECT PAIRING PARTNER:	**Doritos Tangy Cheese**

Brown ales straddle a strange cultural divide: once the traditional working-class beer in the North East of England, brands such as Newcastle Brown have taken on a much more youthful trendiness in export markets around the world. Using predominantly brown malt, as the name suggests, they're not as punchy in flavour as other darker beers, nor are they as carbonated, carrying sweeter, caramel-led and honeyed flavours alongside a touch of nuttiness. There's also quite a distinct lack of bitterness too, meaning you can lean into some stronger flavours of crisps: think malty textures and broad cheesiness to work nicely with the softer, sweeter flavours.

Why This Pairing Works

Doritos – and other tortilla chips – have a slightly rustic, malted note which plays very nicely with the softer notes of the brown ale. The cheesy notes aren't too punchy or overwhelming and the saltiness brings out a sweet nuttiness and a touch of liquorice spice in the beer. A subtle but tasty pairing!

Flavour Groups

Cheesy/Malty/Nutty

Which Brands To Try

Newcastle Brown Ale, Sam Adams Alcohol-Free Brown Ale and Manns Brown Ale (all UK).

Dark Beer

DRINKS GROUP:	**Dark beer**
TYPE:	**Lambic fruit beer**
PERFECT PAIRING PARTNER:	**Cheetos Twisted Sweet & Spicy or Flamin' Hot/black peppercorn and salt crisps**

In all honesty, this pairing filled me with a certain amount of trepidation. Lambic fruit beers from Belgium are wonderfully sweet, aromatic and fragrant, with cherry and raspberry flavours often the most popular, with fruit added into the beer and left to macerate for several months. They deliver an additional crisp, tart note thanks to the wild yeasts used in the brewing process. However, it turns out they're fun to work with from a pairing perspective and the sweetness turns out to be a bit of a superpower. Sweeter spiced snacks are truly joyous when paired with fruit beer, and if you choose a puffed corn snack, you'll find the slightly creamy texture really helps lift some of the fruitiness. Quite a revelation!

If you enjoyed this pairing, you may also like the pairing on page 92 (fruit cider /sea salt and balsamic vinegar crisps).

Why This Pairing Works

The Cheetos have a delicious, soft, sweet spiciness – and almost a fruitiness of their own – which really helps the lighter fragrance of the beer to sing. The heat is also balanced beautifully with the crispness of the beer, and you'll find something different happening with each mouthful. If your beer is strawberry-based, try pairing with black-peppercorn crisps: the spice works wonders with the fresh, tart fruitiness.

Flavour Groups
Sweet/Heat/Spicy/Fruity

Which Brands To Try
Bacchus Cherry Kriekenbeer, Timmerman's Framboise and Früli Strawberry Beer (all Belgium).

DRINKS GROUP:	**Wild card beer**
TYPE:	**Rauchbier (German smoked beer)**
PERFECT PAIRING PARTNER:	**Yorkshire Crisps Sweet Cured Ham & Pickle/Torres Black Truffle Crisps/Mr Trotter's English Mustard Pork Crackling**

A very bold and complex style of beer, Rauchbier is a tremendously distinct category all of its own. The smoky flavour comes from the drying of the malt, which is done in a kiln under which a wood fire is lit, allowing the smoke to rise through and permeate the grains. A process not unlike the production of Islay Scotch whisky (see page 110). The result is a bold and smoky experience on the palate, with a supporting cast of malty sweet and aromatic hoppy notes too. It's little wonder then that you're going to need an equally distinct crisp to power its way through on the palate to work in harmony.

If you enjoyed this pairing, you may also like the pairing on page 105 (Mezcal Old Fashioned/ Smiths Frazzles Crispy Bacon).

Why This Pairing Works

Think big. This style of beer is certainly a step apart from the norm, and a bold, rich meatiness is going to waft back some of the smoke and bring in sweetness. The pickle element in the Yorkshire crisps adds an additional spiciness, and the truffle in the Torres a lovely earthiness. For a total left-field option, consider the genius of a mustard-seasoned pork scratching, which stretches the savoury snack boundaries to new levels!

Flavour Groups

Smoky/Earthy/Meaty/Malty/Heat

Which Brands To Try

Aecht Schlenkerla Weichsel Rotbier (Germany), Rauk Smoked English Beer and Braybrooke Smoked Lager (both UK).

CIDER

Outside of a perfectly chilled pint of beer, it's hard to beat a quality cider in the refreshment stakes. With such broad variety in the pubs these days: from crisp, almost tart, zesty, dry, oak-aged styles, to sweeter, more floral, pear-driven ciders, and, of course, fruit-flavoured offerings, where berries and other orchard fruit take the front seat, there are plenty of fun snack pairings to explore too.

DRINKS GROUP:	**Cider**
TYPE:	**Dry/cask-aged vintage cider**
PERFECT PAIRING PARTNER:	**Mr Trotter's Pork Crackling/ Beerpig Pork Crackling/Perfectly Vegan Lentil Crackling Smoky Bacon**

This pairing really makes me think of a perfect Sunday roast: a loin of pork, expertly trimmed by a butcher, slowly roasting over a bed of vegetables and apple, with a generous amount of dry cider bringing succulence and flavour. Cask-aged vintage ciders tend to be drier in style (thanks to a longer fermentation) and the earthy, tart, zesty notes combine perfectly with a lovely aromatic, vanilla-led oaky sweetness, giving them refreshment, complexity and subtle woody spices. As a pairing, you really can't go wrong with traditional pork scratchings: a soft meaty note and that divine crunch is a match made in heaven with a great chilled glass of vintage cider.

Why This Pairing Works

The apple notes pick out the sweetness in the crackling, alongside a toasted element from the crunchy bits. It's a textural symphony in the mouth too, with the slight fizz from the cider elevating each crunchy bite!

Flavour Groups

Meaty/Fruity/Salty

Which Brands To Try

Henry Westons Vintage Cider, Dunkertons Vintage Organic Cider and Two Orchards Traditional Method Cider (all UK).

DRINKS GROUP:	**Cider**
TYPE:	**Sweet cider**
PERFECT PAIRING PARTNER:	**Walkers BBQ Pork Ribs Crisps/ vegetable crisps**

Sweeter varieties of cider, including rosé, tend to be full of fragrant, brighter, lighter orchard fruit notes, with a wonderful floral structure and softer flavours. They use sweeter varieties of apples that haven't ripened as fully, have lower tannins and a naturally higher sugar content. From a pairing perspective, they work well with barbecue-led flavours, as well as more naturally sweet vegetable-style crisps, including beetroot and parsnip.

Why This Pairing Works
Barbecue flavours tend to be on the sweet/savoury side and have lots of honeyed/maple notes, which pair superbly with the fresh crisp notes in the cider. The fragrant apple also helps to bring out a little more spiciness and the vegetable crisps have a lovely natural sweetness to them, which accents the honey and vanilla flavours in the cider.

Flavour Groups
Sweet/Fruity/Veggie/Meaty

Which Brands To Try
Galipette Rosé Cidre (France), Ridge & Furrow Naturally Sweet Devon Cider (UK) and Orchard Thieves Apple Cider (UK).

Cider

DRINKS GROUP:	**Cider**
TYPE:	**Fruit cider**
PERFECT PAIRING PARTNER:	**Smoky bacon/sea salt and balsamic vinegar/black pepper crisps**

Time for something utterly fruitylicious! Fruit cider is a hugely varied category that tends to be led by greater aromatic, floral, fresh notes, the very best examples adding real fruit juices to the base cider, including blackberry, blackcurrant, raspberry, rhubarb or elderflower. As such, to some purists, they're not really considered to be as complex or made for connoisseurs, but that's not really the point. On a stupendously hot day, the refreshing fruit notes and crisp, zesty apple flavours are very moreish indeed. From a pairing perspective, think similarly to lambic fruit beers (see page 88), where balsamic notes bring out more freshness, and black pepper or smoky bacon is always a winning combination.

Why This Pairing Works

The richer notes in balsamic vinegar really help to develop the softer fruit flavours in raspberry and strawberries – throw in a little black pepper and the slightly piquant notes cut through the layers of sweetness nicely. Similarly, the smoky, meaty notes in any bacon crisp really help to dial up the delicious balance of 'swavoury' in every mouthful.

Flavour Groups

Fruity/Sweet/Smoky/Spicy

Which Brands To Try

Brothers Un-Berrylievable Cider (UK), Rekorderlig Wild Berries Cider (Sweden) and Old Mout Pineapple & Raspberry Alcohol-Free Cider (New Zealand).

GIN COCKTAILS

If gin's your thing (think Negronis, G&Ts and Martinis), you're in for a treat, as the botanical balance of all the great flavours in the spirit (juniper, citrus notes and spice) really lends itself perfectly to crisps. There are also plenty of non-alcoholic alternatives to try too.

DRINKS GROUP:	**Gin cocktails**
TYPE:	**Negroni**
PERFECT PAIRING PARTNER:	**Jacob's Cracker Crisps Sea Salt & Balsamic Vinegar/Kettle Sea Salt & Balsamic Chips**

The Negroni is not only an all-time classic cocktail, but something of a revelation in the world of savoury cocktails. The balance of herbaceous London Dry gin, dry, slightly bitter Campari and sweet vermouth (there's even a non-alcoholic 'No-groni too') isn't everyone's cup of tea, but when made perfectly – in equal parts – it's hard to beat. The drink was supposedly created back in 1919 by Count Camillo Negroni, looking for a punchier version of an Americano cocktail, which used soda water instead of the count's preferred gin. The legend was born, and the rich, complex flavour make it a wonderful drink to pair crisps with. Think simply here: a salty base is really all that's required. Cin cin!

Why This Pairing Works
With a drink so bold in flavour, you don't want to upset the balance too much. The salty notes help to develop the sweetness in the vermouth and the subtle darker twist of the balsamic blends nicely with the dry/earthy notes of the Campari and crisp, herbaceous notes of the juniper in the gin.

Flavour Groups
Salty/Herby/Earthy/Sweet

The Ultimate Negroni Recipe
In a mixing glass or large tumbler, add 30 ml of London Dry gin (regular Beefeater – or the 0.0% version – is hard to beat), 30 ml Campari and 30 ml of sweet vermouth (try Punt e Mes). Add ice and stir for twenty-five seconds. Strain into another tumbler filled with fresh ice and garnish with a large slice of orange.

Gin Cocktails

DRINKS GROUP:	**Gin cocktails**
TYPE:	**Gibson**
PERFECT PAIRING PARTNER:	**Monster Munch Pickled Onion/ Space Raiders Pickled Onion**

While the Martini (page 10?) is arguably the most classy, clean and seriously chic way to drink gin (or vodka, if you're James Bond), its close cousin the Gibson is a wonderfully savoury alternative. Its construction is roughly the same: just gin and dry vermouth, heavier on the gin for a drier style, or more of the vermouth for a wetter, more refreshing cocktail. The main difference is really all in the garnish: instead of the usual olive or twist of lemon peel, the Gibson calls for a tiny silverskin onion – which makes this the perfect drink to partner with everyone's childhood favourite, Monster Munch Pickled Onion, or, if you like slightly less of a pungent punch, a Space Raider.

If you enjoyed this pairing, you may also like the pairing on page 99 (Classic Gin Martini/Brindisa Patatas Sarriegui Crisps).

Why This Pairing Works

Gin is such a savoury-based spirit, and the botanicals are really lifted by anything with a pungent, pickled or piquant flavour. With a herbaceous wash of dry vermouth too, the sharp pickled-onion notes really zing on the palate and the softer crunch gives a lovely texture for the cocktail to land. You'll never look a packet of Monster Munch in the same way, I guarantee it!

Flavour Groups

Oniony/Herby/Zesty/Spicy

The Ultimate Gibson Recipe

In a mixing glass or large tumbler, pour 60 ml of London Dry gin (try No. 3 in this recipe or, for a low-alcohol version, Portobello Road Temperance Spirit) and 20 ml dry vermouth (Noilly Prat), add ice and stir for thirty seconds. Strain into a chilled cocktail glass and garnish with two or three small silverskin onions on a cocktail stick.

DRINKS GROUP:	**Gin cocktails**
TYPE:	**Gin & Tonic**
PERFECT PAIRING PARTNER:	**Asda Extra Special Sea Salt & Chardonnay Wine Vinegar Crisps**

Successful iconic duos last the test of time because of the symbiotic chemistry between both partners, and the Gin & Tonic is probably the greatest liquid partnership of all. Historically, tonic water was designed as a repellent for malaria-carrying mosquitos in India, and the bitter quinine taste became much more palatable when combined with the aromatic beauty of dry gin. The classic sundowner drink had arrived, and the G&T is about as perfect an English duo as you could ever find. So much complexity and refreshment calls for something simple and complementary: a touch of saltiness and the deft zing of a white-wine vinegar are all you need for a heavenly coming together of flavours.

Why This Pairing Works

Very few cocktails are as refreshing as a G&T, and the salty crisp crunch helps the palate open up to layers of complex botanical flavours in the gin and the bittersweet notes of the tonic water. White-wine vinegar gives a lovely acidity to the fizzy mouthfeel and helps to elevate the zestiness of the garnish – either lemon or lime will work. Try switching the gin for a few dashes of Angostura bitters with tonic for a low-alcohol version.

Flavour Groups

Salty/Herby/Zesty/Sweet

The Ultimate G&T Recipe

Take a large wineglass and fill with ice. Add a good double measure of gin (Plymouth is my go-to G&T gin – 50 ml minimum, don't skimp! – or Beefeater 0.0%) and give a quick stir with a bar spoon. Next add 150 ml of chilled tonic water (choose something like Fever Tree or Double Dutch) and stir again. Take a fresh wedge of lemon or lime, give it a quick squeeze and drop in. Perfect!

Gin Cocktails

DRINKS GROUP:	**Gin cocktails**
TYPE:	**Classic Gin Martini**
PERFECT PAIRING PARTNER:	**Tyrrells Mediterranean Herb/ Brindisa Patatas Sarriegui/ Manomasa Manchego & Green Olive Tortilla Chips**

Even though the Martini is one of the simplest cocktails, requiring just two ingredients (OK, ice, a garnish and time, if you're being picky), the level of chic sophistication is hard to beat. First invented in the nineteenth century and really finding fame in the roaring 1920s, it's a boozy drink that beckons, rather than shouts for attention. Best with a luxurious gin and complex dry vermouth, the classic garnishes are either a plump olive or lemon twist. Some like to add in the salty brine from the olive to make a Dirty Martini, but a much classier recipe is to add a few drops of extra-virgin olive oil and a twist. Whatever your pleasure, you'll want something equally classy as a snack and Mediterranean herbs, or anything with salty olives in works an absolute treat.

Why This Pairing Works

Use a more Mediterranean-influenced gin (such as Gin Mare) and you're in savoury heaven here. The Med herbs add some wonderful light fragrance, and the olive-oil crisps give you more complex viscous notes on the palate. Throw in a little rich, nutty continental cheese and you've raised the bar to new heights indeed.

Flavour Groups
Herby/Zesty/Nutty/Earthy/Fruity

The Ultimate Martini Recipe
Take 60 ml Gin Mare, the Botanist (or Warner's Juniper Double Dry non-alcoholic) and 15 ml dry vermouth and stir over ice for twenty-five to thirty seconds. Strain into a chilled cocktail glass and add three or four drops of olive oil onto the surface of the drink. Garnish with a thin piece of lemon peel.

TEQUILA AND MEZCAL COCKTAILS

Tequila-based drinks – perhaps the ultimate party-starter of a spirit – have herbaceous, savoury notes perfect for pairing.

DRINKS GROUP:	**Tequila and mezcal cocktails**
TYPE:	**Paloma**
PERFECT PAIRING PARTNER:	**Walkers Max Strong Jalapeño & Cheese/Real Handcooked Jalapeño Pepper Crisps**

The Paloma is a wonderfully effervescent and stylish Mexican cocktail which can be enjoyed by anyone who is – or isn't – a tequila fan. Its refreshing burst of pink-grapefruit zestiness, tart fresh lime, and herbaceous silver – or reposado – tequila is a flavour combo perfect for weekend grazing brunches, or to start the night with an effervescent bang. One of the great things is that it gives a platform for a quality tequila to really stand out and the vegetal notes take on a sightly sweeter role alongside the pink-grapefruit soda (which is now, fortunately, widely available). From a pairing perspective, something fruity, salty and a touch cheesy works really well.

Why This Pairing Works
The sweet, slightly tart note of the grapefruit soda offers a nice counterpoint to the saltiness and all-round punch of the cheese here, and the slightly warm, vegetal notes in the jalapeño really bring out the freshness of the lime and the overall savoury/herbaceous flavours of the tequila.

Flavour Groups
Cheesy/Herby/Heat/Spicy/Sweet

The Ultimate Paloma Recipe
In a tall, slender glass full of ice cubes, add 50 ml of quality tequila (1800 or Patron reposado work well, or seek out Lyre's non-alcoholic Agave Blanco) and the juice of half a fresh lime. Stir briefly, then top up with pink-grapefruit soda (Fever Tree or Three Cents are great). Garnish with a lime or pink grapefruit wedge.

DRINKS GROUP:	**Tequila and mezcal cocktails**
TYPE:	**Margarita**
PERFECT PAIRING PARTNER:	**Takis Fuego Hot Chilli Pepper & Lime Corn Snacks**

If you're looking for a ray of Mexico sunshine, then look no further than a Margarita. This heavenly coming together of silver or reposado (slightly aged) tequila, lime and orange liqueur will sizzle and salsa across the palate from the start of the evening till sunrise. There are plenty of variants to try if you're looking for a twist too: spicier varieties with a dash of hot sauce (Picante), sweeter versions ('Tommy's', with agave syrup) and frozen, blitzed up in a blender. The cooling, refreshing, herbaceous-sweet notes, tart lime and intense zesty orange are fabulous when paired with anything spicy, especially the tumultuous tubes of terror, Takis.

If you enjoyed this pairing, you may also like the pairing on page 122 (Daiquiri / Yorkshire Crisps Sweet Chilli & Lime)

Why This Pairing Works

Classic Margs are full of life and the cooling, softer herby notes bring a cleansing balance to the intensely spicy notes of the Takis: you'll find an almost creamy, soothing feel on the palate, with the lime from the crisp bringing out more zestiness and the punchy chilli amplifying the heat. A devilishly good combo indeed!

Flavour Groups

Spicy/Herby/Heat/Veggie/Zesty/Sweet

The Ultimate Margarita Recipe

In a cocktail shaker add 50 ml reposado tequila (Patrón is perfect, or Almave non-alcoholic agave spirit), 25 ml fresh lime juice, 20 ml orange liqueur (Cointreau is the classic) and a tiny pinch of salt. Shake for fifteen to twenty seconds and strain into an ice-filled tumbler. Garnish with a slice of fresh lime.

DRINKS GROUP:	**Tequila and mezcal cocktails**
TYPE:	**Bloody Maria**
PERFECT PAIRING PARTNER:	**Doritos Chilli Heatwave/ Manomasa Serrano Chilli & Yucatan Honey Tortilla Chips**

The Bloody Maria is a Mexican 'twist' on the Bloody Mary, the undisputed spicy, savoury vodka-based classic. However, it's far more than simply a variant: in my opinion it's an improvement on the original, and the addition of herbaceous, vegetal tequila brings something even more exciting to the party. Half the joy with this style of cocktail is just how outlandish the garnish can be, and a quick Google reveals exactly how far some drinkers are willing to push the envelope: crispy bacon slices, grilled cocktail sausages and other savoury snacks often feature alongside the typical celery stick and cherry tomatoes. So, given the symbiotic snacking potential, pairing the Bloody Maria with any bold chips such as tortillas will work an absolute treat.

If you enjoyed this pairing, you may also like the pairing on page 116 (Bloody Mary/Twiglets).

Why This Pairing Works
As the Bloody Maria already brings heat, you could argue that too much would be a bad thing, however the saucy/tomato notes in the chips bring a touch of sweetness to the savoury, herbaceous spice and the rustic corn feel, and crunch is a perfect foundation for munching on any ostentatious garnish.

Flavour Groups
Spicy/Heat/Herby/Veggie/Sweet

The Ultimate Bloody Maria Recipe
In a tall glass add 50 ml blanco or silver tequila, such as Olmeca Altos, or non-alcoholic agave spirit, two dashes of hot sauce (my favourite is Cholula or Valentina Muy Picante), three dashes of Worcestershire sauce, half a beef stock cube, crumbled (optional), and a generous grind of salt and black pepper. Stir until the stock cube has dissolved, then add cubed ice and 100 ml of tomato juice. Stir again to lift all the flavours and garnish with a couple of cherry tomatoes, a small lemon wedge and an olive.

DRINKS GROUP:	**Tequila and mezcal cocktails**
TYPE:	**Mezcal Old Fashioned**
PERFECT PAIRING PARTNER:	**Salted roasted pecan nuts/Smiths Bacon Fries/Smiths Frazzles Crispy Bacon**

The Old Fashioned (see page 113 for more history) is, in many ways, the daddy of all cocktails, and its versatility has led it to be a great vehicle for other spirits too. Enter mezcal: tequila's smoky, rustic hermano from the south of Mexico. Mezcal has become very on-trend recently, thanks to its distinct, pungent smoky aroma and warming sweet-herbal flavour and it's these qualities which make it work well in an Old Fashioned, bringing sweetness, spice and zesty fruity aromas too. When pairing it with a snack, think about enhancing the smokiness, with sweet, salty bacon notes, or bringing some wildcard nuttiness into the mix.

If you enjoyed this pairing, you may also like the pairing on page 111 (Old Fashioned/barbecue chips)

Why This Pairing Works

Another non-crisp suggestion here, but what the hell... it really works! The sweet, salty and roasted notes of the pecans help to balance the smoke-driven flavours of the mezcal with the sweetness of the rest of the drink. Also, the bacon notes and texture of the Frazzles or Bacon Fries bring another elevated waft of sweet smoke to the drink.

Flavour Groups
Smoky/Sweet/Nutty/Meaty/Salty

The Ultimate Mezcal Old Fashioned Recipe

In a tumbler, add one teaspoon of soft muscovado sugar and a dash of water. Stir to dissolve. Next add 50 ml mezcal (try Ojo de Dios), a dash of Angostura bitters, a dash of black walnut bitters (optional) and cubed ice. Stir slowly for thirty seconds, add a few more cubes, and then garnish with a thin piece of orange zest.

WHISK(E)Y COCKTAILS

From smooth Irish whiskeys and fruity American bourbon to robust, smoky Scotch whiskies, there's a crisp pairing just waiting to be discovered.

DRINKS GROUP:	**Whisk(e)y cocktails**
TYPE:	**Highball**
PERFECT PAIRING PARTNER:	**Kettle Sea Salt & Crushed Black Peppercorn Chips/Smiths Scampi Fries/Proper Barbecue Lentil Chips**

Whisky is a spirit very close to my heart, and the sheer variety of styles can bedazzle the palate and adapt to almost any social gathering. From bold and smoky single malt Scotch whiskies from the island of Islay, sumptuous complex blends, to light and refreshing Irish whiskeys and more spicy and rich whiskies from Japan – and now India – there's really a style for everyone, despite any misgivings! The Highball is also the perfect vehicle to show off that flavoursome versatility, bringing great refreshment too. When pairing, think about the headline style of the whisk(e)y: if it has smokiness, bring in something peppery or even slightly fishy to bring out the notes. For smoother styles (such as Irish), think lighter, more delicate flavours.

Why This Pairing Works

I like using a blended Scotch or smoky single malt in a Highball, and the black pepper really helps to not only bring out the smoke a touch, but also some sweetness in the whisky. The salty notes also help to develop the briny flavours and aromas. Try also pairing a Laphroaig or Ardbeg (neat or on the rocks) with Scampi Fries for the ultimate coastal delight. The whole experience is wonderfully complex and very moreish! Sláinte!

Flavour Groups

Smoky/Salty/Spicy/Earthy/Zesty

The Ultimate Highball Recipe

Take a tall glass and add 50 ml of whisky (my choice would be a complex blend like Johnnie Walker Black Label or Ardray) and fill with ice. Pour over 150–200 ml chilled soda water and stir to mix properly. Garnish with a thin piece of lemon zest.

DRINKS GROUP:	# Whisk(e)y cocktails
TYPE:	## Penicillin
PERFECT PAIRING PARTNER:	## Walkers Sensations Thai Sweet Chilli/Tyrrells Sweet Chilli & Red Pepper Crisps

The Penicillin is not one of the best-known whisky-based cocktails, but from a flavour perspective it's one of the true greats and a wonderful drink to banish the winter blues. Not dissimilar to a Hot Toddy (although it's served over ice), it brings together blended Scotch whisky, a touch of smoky single malt, fresh lemon juice, ginger liqueur and honey – all big, bold flavours indeed, but when combined it's something that will keep the sniffles at bay. It's also a very easy drink to make and works well with spicy flavours, so you can go to town with your snack pairing.

Why This Pairing Works

Despite being a cold cocktail, you'll get a warming feeling in the mouth thanks to the ginger, which is really complimented by the sweet-chilli notes and light heat of the crisp. Any smoky flavours also work nicely with the other spices in the crisp, and the whole experience is an explosion of warmth and delight.

Flavour Groups

Spicy/Zesty/Heat/Sweet./Smoky

The Ultimate Penicillin Recipe

Add 45 ml of blended Scotch to a shaker along with 15 ml smoky single malt, such as Laphroaig. Next add 20 ml honey syrup (a mix of 2:1 water to runny honey), 15 ml ginger liqueur (King's Ginger Liqueur is ideal), and 20 ml freshly squeezed lemon juice. Fill with ice and shake for twelve to fifteen seconds, straining into an ice-filled tumbler. Garnish with a piece of crystallised ginger.

DRINKS GROUP:	**Whisk(e)y cocktails**
TYPE:	**Irish Whiskey & Cola**
PERFECT PAIRING PARTNER:	**Tayto Smoky Bacon Crisps**

Sometimes the simplest pairings are unbeatable – and a generous pour of sweet and fruity Irish whiskey over ice, topped up with cola, is terrific, especially during long summer weekends. Irish whiskey tends to be more on the lighter side of the flavour spectrum, with sweeter, vanilla-led notes and tropical fruit, so works nicely as a base for simple-yet-delicious long drinks. From a pairing perspective, anything smoky-bacon-led will work here (try them, or barbecue-flavoured crisps, with just the cola for a non-alcoholic pairing), but the best ones are really Ireland's finest, Tayto!

Why This Pairing Works
Cola and bacon crisps are already a delicious pairing (call it the Smoky Cokey if you like...) and the sweeter oakiness and vanilla-led flavours of the Irish whiskey really gels the whole thing together, giving it some additional complexity and lighter, fruitier notes.

Flavour Groups
Sweet/Smoky/Meaty

Which Brands to Try Mixing with Cola
Jameson Caskmates, Bushmills Blackbush and Teeling Small Batch Irish Whiskey (all Ireland).

DRINKS GROUP:	**Whisk(e)y cocktails**
TYPE:	**Old Fashioned**
PERFECT PAIRING PARTNER:	**Lay's Barbecue Chips/Popchips Barbeque**

The perfect meeting point of sweet, spicy and spirit: as the OG in the world of cocktails, the Old Fashioned was supposedly created in the US during the mid-nineteenth century, bringing together sugar, water, bitters and American whiskey, although it can probably trace its roots to an even earlier period in US history. When it was invented really isn't important, though: today it's still one of the most popular drinks in the world and brings a level of incredible balance and sophistication into the glass with just three key ingredients. As an all-American classic, think about pairing this with the sweet, spicy and meaty notes of an all-American BBQ and you'll be smiling from ear to ear in delight!

Why This Pairing Works

The charred sweetcorn notes, vanilla, caramel and fruitiness of the bourbon in the cocktail are a perfect partner for the sweeter, spicier notes in the barbecue chips, and the saltiness also helps to cut through the incredibly rich, thick mouthfeel. The lighter, crispier texture of the Popchips brings a different quality too.

Flavour Groups

Sweet/Spicy/Meaty/Fruity/Zesty

The Ultimate Old Fashioned Recipe

In a tumbler add a teaspoon of maple syrup, 50 ml of bourbon (Four Roses, Maker's Mark and Woodford Reserve are excellent) and two dashes of Angostura bitters. Add ice and stir for twenty to thirty seconds until the ice has diluted it slightly. Add a few more cubes, and garnish with a slice of fresh orange.

DRINKS GROUP:	**Whisk(e)y cocktails**
TYPE:	**Manhattan**
PERFECT PAIRING PARTNER:	**Sea salt and balsamic vinegar crisps**

Another classic American cocktail with a highly complex flavour and sophisticated feel, the Manhattan hails from the same golden age of drinks as the Martini: big, bold, boozy concoctions, but with incredible subtleties when you delve in deeper. Bringing together American whiskey (usually bourbon), sweet vermouth and bitters, you can tailor it personally to your liking by adding in some herbaceous dry vermouth too – a Perfect Manhattan is an equal mix of the two. Given the depth of flavours here, you don't want anything too big to swamp the complexity, and so a simple, salty snack with a touch of sweetness, such as rich balsamic vinegar, will be ideal.

Why This Pairing Works

Manhattans can be a real handful on the palate, with sweetness coming from the vermouth and bourbon, and layers of woody, earthy spiciness also present, alongside fresh acidity and dark fruit from the cherry and orange-zest garnishes. A solid crunchy texture is needed, with saltiness to cut through the sweetness, the balsamic bringing a real zing to the party too.

Flavour Groups

Sweet/Spicy/Earthy/Salty/Zesty/ Fruity

The Perfect Manhattan Recipe

In a mixing glass add 50 ml of bourbon (Maker's Mark or Woodford Reserve), two dashes of Angostura bitters, 15 ml sweet vermouth and 15 ml of dry vermouth. Add ice and stir for thirty seconds. Strain into a chilled cocktail glass and garnish with a thin slice of orange peel and two cocktail cherries on a cocktail stick.

VODKA COCKTAILS

Vodka is a great spirit to add some punch to almost any cocktail – so the following pairings are all about the diverse flavours you can play with.

DRINKS GROUP:	# Vodka cocktails
TYPE:	# Bloody Mary
PERFECT PAIRING PARTNER:	# Twiglets/Pringles Sour Cream & Onion/Seabrook Worcestershire Sauce Crisps

Queen of the savoury cocktails, the Bloody Mary is perhaps as misunderstood as it is loved. To some it's like cold tomato soup: lifeless and undrinkable, but to others (including me) it's virtually a meal in a glass. What's intriguing is that it can be tweaked endlessly until perfection ensues: the ratio of hot sauce to Worcestershire sauce, celery salt, horseradish, stock cubes and all this before we get to the garnish. Really the vodka is there as an alcoholic accoutrement (you can simply have an equally delicious Virgin Mary without vodka), and I personally prefer the Bloody Maria (see page 106), which calls for tequila. Either way, it's a delightful cocktail to pair snacks to and you can twist it in many ways: sour cream and onion are particularly effective, alongside the meaty/yeasty delights of the Twiglet.

If you enjoyed this pairing, you may also like the pairing on page 104 (Bloody Maria/Doritos Chilli Heatwave).

Why This Pairing Works

The creaminess really doesn't get in the way of any of the other flavours involved: it acts as a base on which everything can build nicely, with a little twang of onion building up the savoury notes. Similarly, Twiglets bring an additional meatiness, which pairs wonderfully with the rich tomato notes and heat. The additional Worcestershire sauce flavours just hype up the tomato and spice balance to great effect!

Flavour Groups

Spicy/Heat/Creamy/Oniony/Meaty

The Perfect Bloody Mary Recipe

In a tall glass, add 50 ml vodka (I usually use Eight Lands or Belvedere), a grind of black pepper and salt, three dashes of hot sauce (Frank's or Tabasco), three dashes of Worcestershire sauce, half a teaspoon of horseradish sauce, and a pinch of celery salt. Stir to mix, then add ice and 200 ml of tomato juice. Stir again to lift the flavours and garnish with a celery stick.

DRINKS GROUP:	**Vodka cocktails**
TYPE:	**Espresso Martini**
PERFECT PAIRING PARTNER:	**ParmCrisps Original Parmesan/ Whisps Parmesan Crisps/M&S Cheese Straws**

Ah, the Espresso Martini. This potent elixir of Soho in the 1980s was created by British bartending legend Dick Bradsell in response to an unnamed supermodel wanting a drink to 'wake me up and f**k me up'. The real protagonist of the story will forever remain a secret, as its creator sadly passed away in 2016. Either way, it's a great story and the drink is still proving to be a potent classic – arguably the UK's favourite cocktail, in fact. One social media trend saw people grating Parmesan cheese into their drink, which, let's be realistic, is a truly awful idea. However, it got me thinking about it as a snack combo – and lo and behold... the flavours actually work together!

Why This Pairing Works

The bittersweet coffee notes are really highlighted by the tart, sharp, salty creaminess of the cheese and the darker, more complex earthy notes start to come alive. I know you won't believe me, but it's true!

Flavour Groups

Cheesy/Earthy/Salty/Sweet

The Perfect Espresso Martini Recipe

In a shaker add 50 ml vodka, 30 ml freshly brewed espresso coffee, 20 ml coffee liqueur (Kahlúa or Mr Black) and a dash of sugar syrup to taste, and vigorously shake for twenty seconds. Strain into a cocktail glass and garnish with three coffee beans on the frothy surface of the drink.

DRINKS GROUP:	**Vodka cocktails**
TYPE:	**Cosmopolitan**
PERFECT PAIRING PARTNER:	**Manomasa Green Lemon & Pink Peppercorn Tortilla Chips/ Walkers Sensations Crushed Sea Salt & Black Peppercorn Crisps**

Like the Espresso Martini, the Cosmo is a modern classic, and its layers of crisp fruitiness and citrus twang have refreshed the palates of partygoers and casual diners since it became popular in the 1980s. The secret to its success is arguably how nicely balanced each element is together (vodka, cranberry juice, fresh lime and Cointreau) but also that it's particularly easy to drink and has plenty of delicious variants and serves: straight up, extra fruity (with fresh berries) over ice, or even frozen – the 'Frozmopolitan'. When it comes to snacks, the fruitiness might give cause for concern, but fret not: a waft of peppery spice really works wonders, much in the same way that strawberries and black pepper is truly a pairing from the gods.

Why This Pairing Works

The crisp maltiness of the tortillas bring a lovely substance to the drink and the lighter, slightly more fragrant notes of the pink peppercorns help to define the fruitiness and citrus punch. If you prefer things a little heavier, the black peppercorn notes bring out a crisp dryness from the cranberry and Cointreau.

Flavour Groups

Fruity/Spicy/Zesty

The Perfect Cosmo Recipe

In a cocktail shaker, add 45 ml of vodka (you can use a citrus-flavoured vodka, or plain), 15 ml Cointreau, 30 ml of cranberry juice and 10 ml of freshly squeezed lime juice. Shake for fifteen to twenty seconds and strain into a cocktail glass. Garnish with a small piece of lemon zest.

DRINKS GROUP:	**Vodka cocktails**
TYPE:	**Porn Star Martini**
PERFECT PAIRING PARTNER:	**Tyrrells Posh Prawn Cocktail Crisps/Prawn Cocktail Skips**

As drinks titles go, the Porn Star Martini is arguably one of the cheekiest, and with its combination of passion fruit, vanilla vodka and lime juice alongside a separate chilled shot of sparkling wine, it's certainly one of the most fun-filled cocktails. Another modern classic – from the early 2000s created by London bartending legend, the late Douglas Ankrah – the Porn Star or Passion Fruit Martini has little by way of a resemblance to a traditional Martini, but who cares: it's an exhilarating way to start the night, and there are very few drinks which can really get the party going quite like it. The bold, tropical-fruit flavours aren't the easiest thing to pair other flavours with, but lighter, sweeter shellfish are a big yes.

Why This Pairing Works

The sweet, slightly spiced tomato and shellfish notes blend surprisingly well with the bold fruitiness of the fresh passion fruit in the cocktail, and the softer texture of the Skips makes for a lighter, more well-rounded mouthfeel, especially with the additional sparkling wine.

Flavour Groups

Fruity/Sweet/Fishy/Spicy/Zesty

The Perfect Porn Star Martini Recipe

In a shaker, add half a fresh passion fruit, 40 ml vanilla vodka (Stoli), 20 ml Passoã passion-fruit liqueur, 10 ml fresh lime juice and a dash of sugar syrup. Shake for fifteen to twenty seconds and strain into a cocktail glass. Garnish with the other half of passion fruit and fill a shot glass with chilled Prosecco, which can be poured in separately.

RUM COCKTAILS

*The taste of sunshine!
Rum brings a tropical
delight to cocktails and
is great to pair similarly
colourful flavours to.*

DRINKS GROUP:	**Rum cocktails**
TYPE:	**Daiquiri**
PERFECT PAIRING PARTNER:	**Yorkshire Crisps Sweet Chilli & Lime/The Dormen Sweet Chilli & Lime Crisps**

If you want to find out the true skill of a bartender, ask them to make you a classic rum Daiquiri. Despite the three basic ingredients (light rum, fresh lime juice and sugar syrup), the perfect balance between them is an art to perfect, even down to whether one should leave in the small shards of ice after straining or sieve them out. It's a skill that, once mastered, will give you a staggeringly delicious drink time and time again, full of fresh, zesty headiness and a lovely mix of earthy and floral notes. Pairing anything lime-flavour-based will work here, especially when bringing in a little heat and spice to the party as well.

Why This Pairing Works

Classic Daiquiris are among the freshest, cleanest cocktails, so a little zing of chilli heat really adds to the experience, and with an additional hit of zesty lime, alongside the slightly oily crunch of a well-fried potato slice, the combination is utterly delicious.

Flavour Groups

Heat/Spicy/Zesty/Fruity

The Perfect Daiquiri Recipe

In a cocktail shaker add 50 ml light rum (Havana Club 3 Year Old works perfectly), 15 ml freshly squeezed lime juice, 10 ml sugar syrup and a dash (half a teaspoon) of Cointreau. Shake vigorously for fifteen to twenty seconds and strain into a cocktail glass. Garnish with a slice of lime.

DRINKS GROUP:	**Rum cocktails**
TYPE:	**Mojito**
PERFECT PAIRING PARTNER:	**McCoy's Thai Sweet Chicken/ Pipers Wild Thyme & Rosemary Crisps**

What time is it? It's Mojito o'clock! This incredibly refreshing Cuban classic isn't dissimilar to the Daiquiri in terms of its ingredients, but of course brings in the herbaceous delight of fresh mint to pep up the palate, alongside sparkling water to lengthen the experience. As summer cocktails go, a well-made Mojito is a real zinger, and the delicious earthy and floral rum notes, zesty lime and fragrant mint are wonderful to pair with anything heady, aromatic and spicy, such as Thai-style spices and lighter herby crisps, such as rosemary, thyme and vegetable crisps.

Why This Pairing Works

This pairing is all about the combined brilliance of the aromas: the herby/sweet fragrance of the fresh mint leaves combines nicely with the lighter spicy notes of the Thai-influenced flavours in the McCoy's as well as the garden notes of the rosemary and thyme. The lime in the Mojito cuts through the heavier fattiness of the crisps too.

Flavour Groups

Herby/Zesty/Spicy/Sweet

The Perfect Mojito Recipe

In a tall glass, add a handful of fresh mint leaves, 50 ml light rum (such as Havana Club 3 Year Old, or for a spiced non-alcoholic version, CleanCo Clean R rum alternative), 10 ml fresh lime juice, 10 ml sugar syrup and a little crushed ice. Muddle the mixture together using the flat end of a bar spoon, then add more crushed ice and top up with chilled sparkling water. Garnish with a sprig of mint and a fresh lime wedge and give a final stir.

OTHER COCKTAILS

*Let's get our party
swagger on and take
a look at how the
complexity and richness
of other cocktails
can pair well with a
selection of fine savoury
snacking delights.*

DRINKS GROUP:	**Other cocktails**
TYPE:	**Aperol Spritz**
PERFECT PAIRING PARTNER:	**M&S Italian Style Pancetta Crisps/Brindisa Patatas Sarriegui/Torres Extra Virgin Olive Oil/balsamic vinegar and sea salt crisps**

Now a modern-day classic, the Aperol Spritz has blitzed its way into homes and sun-drenched gardens across the UK, helping to cement our love for the aperitif – and the aperitivo hour. Aperol was first created in 1919 in Padua in Northern Italy and on its own, the fruity, dry flavours are reminiscent of its other Italian counterpart, Campari. But lift it with Prosecco, a touch of soda water – and occasionally, a cheeky splash of gin – and its bittersweet, effervescent charms come out to play. It pairs beautifully with almost anything from olives, roasted nuts and charcuterie to salt and vinegar crisps, so you can really go to town without overthinking your snackstravaganza.

If you enjoyed this pairing, you may also like the pairing on page 57 (Prosecco/M&S Prosciutto & Formaggio Crisps).

Why This Pairing Works

The fizzy, fruity, herbaceous and bittersweet notes in Aperol are lifted even further with a touch of salt from the meatiness of actual pancetta crisps or the more intense attack of sea salt. Throw in the sweet bite of balsamic and an unctuous coating of olive oil alongside the crunch for additional smiles.

Flavour Groups

Herby/Meaty/Salty/Sweet

The Perfect Aperol Spritz Recipe

In a large wine glass, add 60 ml of Aperol, 10 ml gin (optional) and ice cubes. Stir briefly, then add 100 ml Prosecco and 20 ml soda water. Stir again to lift the flavours and garnish with a slice of fresh orange.

DRINKS GROUP:	**Other cocktails**
TYPE:	**Brandy Sparkler**
PERFECT PAIRING PARTNER:	**Torres Black Truffle/Tyrrells Truffle & Sea Salt Crisps**

As decadent drinks go, this effervescent brandy-based cocktail, as we shall call it, is right up there as a most elegant sipper. Bringing together rich, effervescent sparkling wine, fruity, vanilla-led oakiness from a great French brandy (think Cognac or Armagnac), brown sugar and a dash of aromatic bitters, it's a great way to lift the start of a dinner party and bring a touch of class to your evening ahead. French brandies like Cognac and Armagnac come from a range of grape varieties and are turned into a grape spirit before being aged in French oak casks to develop layers of sweet spice and delicate fruit notes. The longer they age, the more complex flavours they develop and pairing something with bold flavours like truffle really brings out the very best in all the ingredients.

Why This Pairing Works

Truffle notes tend to be earthy and dry, and this helps heighten the spice and fruit of the brandy, while the delicate fizz of the sparkling wine really cuts through any heavy fattiness in the mouth, the dusting of sea salt also sets off the subtle creaminess in the wine. A bon vivant's pairing and no mistake.

Flavour Groups
Earthy/Fruity/Spicy/Zesty

The Perfect Brandy Sparkler Recipe

In a Champagne flute, add a touch of brown-sugar syrup and a dash of aromatic bitters. Then add 25 ml of Cognac or Armagnac, stir and top up the flute with sparkling wine (my suggestion would be French Crémant). Garnish with a fresh raspberry or small piece of lemon peel.

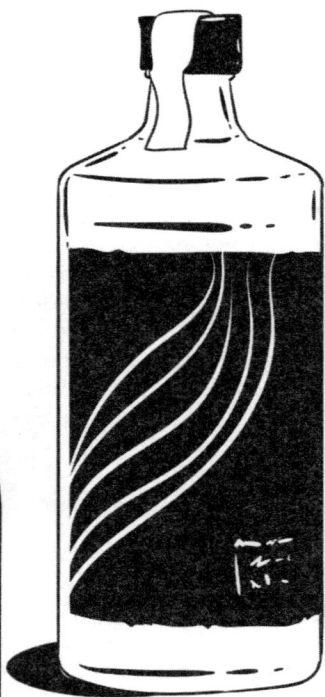

INTERESTING WORLD DRINKS

From dry and earthy to floral, spicy and zesty, these flavoursome pairings from around the world will absolutely tantalise the tastebuds.

DRINKS GROUP:	**Interesting world drinks**
TYPE:	**Saké**
PERFECT PAIRING PARTNER:	**Kettle Asian Chilli Beef Chips/ Monster Munch Sweet & Spicy Flamin' Hot**

Saké, often likened to a rice wine, is actually one of the oldest recorded alcoholic drinks – dating back to around 500 BCE. Drunk either chilled or slightly warmed, saké is brewed rather like a beer, using polished rice grains (to give a cleaner, more fruity taste), and it ferments to an unusually high strength (around 20 per cent ABV) before it is diluted – sometimes it has a small amount of neutral spirit added for additional complexity. You'll find the flavours range from fresh and floral, with orchard fruits, all the way to quite earthy and dry notes, making it a great pairing to grilled meats and bolder, spice-led cuisine: especially red chilli. It is especially enriching to explore the huge range of flavours on offer as part of a full Japanese dining experience.

Why This Pairing Works

While the heat is moderate, the chilli beef crisps bring a lovely salty-sweet savoury note alongside the meatiness of the beef flavour, helping to highlight some of the fresher, more fruity notes in the saké. Throw in the sweeter spice of the Monster Munch and each mouthful takes on a livelier, fun-fuelled ride.

Flavour Groups

Heat/Sweet/Spicy/Earthy/Fruity

Which Brands To Try

SoGood Saké (a Californian take on saké), Four Fox Saké (Japan) and Sawanotsuru Deluxe Saké (Japan).

DRINKS GROUP:	**Interesting world drinks**
TYPE:	**Aquavit**
PERFECT PAIRING PARTNER:	**Pipers Jalapeño & Dill Crisps/ Estrella Dill Chips/Oh My Hog! Salt & Vinegar Pork Crunch**

Aquavit is the spirited star of Scandinavia – with particularly strong roots in Norway and Denmark, where its herbaceous, spice-laden flavours have found favour as a pungent shot during and after mealtimes. At its heart is a complex blend of botanicals, with the caraway seed and dill being the most popular lead flavours. You'll find similarities with gin, with a more savoury element making aquavit a real gem to pair with all sorts of food: from salted, fatty meats such as smoked ham, to anything pickled. One other wonderful element to Aquavit comes during the maturation process: some aquavit barrels are actually taken onboard a ship and sailed down to the equator and back, developing a lovely, nutty, spicy oakiness.

Why This Pairing Works

The dill notes of the crisps work in perfect partnership with the more savoury, vegetal elements of the aquavit, and the slightly sharper pickled heat from the jalapeño brings a delicious, complex aftertaste. Similarly, the fatty crunch of a pork rind balances beautifully with all that herbaceous goodness.

Flavour Groups

Veggie/Meaty/Heat/Spicy

Which Brands To Try

Linie Aquavit (Norway), Copenhagen Distillery Organic Aquavit (Denmark) and Bareksten Spirits Aquavit (Norway).

DRINKS GROUP:	**Interesting world drinks**
TYPE:	**Pisco**
PERFECT PAIRING PARTNER:	**Walkers Sensations Roasted Chicken & Thyme/Char-grilled Chimichurri Crisps/McCoy's Sizzling King Prawn Crisps**

For this fabulous pairing we're going to jump on a plane to South America, making two gastronomic stops: firstly, to Peru and then to Chile. Pisco is the national spirit of both countries – there's been many a late-night debate as to where it developed first – and it's impossible to ignore just how wonderfully flavoursome it truly is. Distilled from a selection of different grape varieties, both aromatic and non-aromatic, pisco has a wonderful orchard fruitiness, alongside darker, richer, spicy notes. Whip it up into a classic Pisco Sour with fresh lime, sugar syrup, egg white (or aquafaba) and bitters, or enjoy it simply with tonic, and pair it with anything from spicy barbecued meat crisps or fragrant shellfish flavours.

Why This Pairing Works
Pisco has a broad spectrum of styles, meaning that it is a spirit suited for plenty of pairings. The slight spice and meatiness of chimichurri steak brings out the fresher side to pisco, and the king prawn helps to heighten a slightly sweeter, more citrus-led note.

Flavour Groups
Sweet/Spicy/Fishy/Meaty/Fruity

Which Brands To Try
Barsol Primera Quebranta (Peru), Waqar Pisco (Chile) and Campo De Encanto Acholado (Peru).

DRINKS GROUP:	**Interesting world drinks**
TYPE:	**Shochu and Soju**
PERFECT PAIRING PARTNER:	**Koikeya Wasabi Nori/Tesco Roast Beef & Horseradish Crisps**

Not unlike saké, shochu has recently become a more widely appreciated drink outside of Japan, and Western consumers have begun to really enjoy its more savoury, almost umami dryness, especially in culinary settings. Shochu is a rice-based distilled spirit, which is first fermented with koji, a specific mould, before it is turned into a very characterful, fresh spirit: full of ripe floral fruitiness, a moderately dry aftertaste and nicely highlighted citrus notes. Soju is a colourless Korean spirit made from rice (but also tapioca and potato), which is not unlike a lower-strength vodka, sometimes infused with fruit flavourings, or enjoyed as a shot with a beer. It's a little-known fact that soju is actually one of the biggest-selling spirits in the world, thanks to just one brand called Jinro. Both spirits pair well with Japanese- or Korean-inspired cuisine, especially pickled vegetables, seafood and teriyaki dishes.

Why This Pairing Works
The more delicate freshness of the shochu is beautifully accented by the slight heat and saltiness of the wasabi and nori seaweed crisps, helping to bring in an almost apple fruitiness, a touch of root vegetable and a nice nutty aftertaste. It's a similarly delicious experience with the roast beef and horseradish, and the meaty, piquant notes bring out a fresh melon and honeyed note in the shochu. The more neutral notes in the soju simply help to dial up the meaty elements of the crisp, alongside a more developed pickle-like flavour too. Unusual, but very good indeed.

Flavour Groups
Heat/Spicy/Earthy/Fruity/Veggie

Which Brands To Try
Toyonaga Honkaku Shochu (Japan), Otogo Ginjo Kuma Shochu (Japan) and Jinro Soju (Korea).

NON-ALCOHOLIC DRINKS

*What to drink
(and pair with) when
you're not drinking!*

DRINKS GROUP:	**Non-alcoholic drinks**
TYPE:	**Ginger Beer**
PERFECT PAIRING PARTNER:	**Walkers Sensations Lime & Coriander Chutney Poppadoms**

As a child, I always saw ginger beer as just that little bit rebellious. It had some bite and a touch of heat, and felt strangely adventurous to ten-year-old me. Nowadays, if I'm out and not drinking alcohol, I'll usually ask for a glass of ginger beer, dependent on the brand behind the bar, and I get the same little fizzle of excitement that I used to. Proper botanically brewed ginger beer shouldn't be too fizzy or sweet, and its punchy, earthy heat pairs wonderfully well with lime especially, and other botanical spices such as coriander, so if you're looking for an exciting masterclass in the mouth, then this is hard to beat.

Why This Pairing Works

The texture of the poppadoms is wonderful with fizzy soft drinks and, after the initial crunch, it gives a slightly softer, creamy base for the ginger and spices to play upon. The heat blends beautifully with the citrus notes of the coriander and, of course, the lime. My new favourite non-alcoholic pairing? A great big zingy yes indeed!

Flavour Groups

Heat/Sweet/Spicy/Earthy/Zesty/Herby

Which Brands To Try

Fentimans (UK), Cawston Press (UK) and Bundaberg (Australia).

DRINKS GROUP:	**Non-alcoholic drinks**
TYPE:	**Orangina**
PERFECT PAIRING PARTNER:	**Lay's 3D Bacon Bugles/Walkers Southern Style BBQ Bugles (if you can't find the Lay's version)**

So, this pairing is, in all honesty, borne out of the insistence of my eldest daughter, Lois. We discovered it purely by chance on a trip to La Rochelle last year, where the supermarkets are filled with unusual varieties of crisp and the fridges stuffed with bottles of Orangina. Many bags of bacon Bugles were consumed poolside during that holiday, washed down with the iconic orange sensation, and to keep the memory of a great trip alive, we came back with a car-boot load of both. It's still Lois's favourite pairing and she would disown me if I left it out of the book, so here it is. Bon vacation!

Why This Pairing Works

The slight smokiness of the crisp really starts to sing with the bittersweet citrus notes of the Orangina, and the whole thing ends up like wonderfully barbecued fruit on the palate. Because Orangina isn't too sweet, it highlights the more honeyed notes in the Bugles too.

Flavour Groups

Sweet/Smoky/Zesty/Fruity

Which Brands To Try

You could try it with Fanta or San Pellegrino, but my colours are nailed firmly to the Orangina mast!

DRINKS GROUP:	**Non-alcoholic drinks**
TYPE:	**Kombucha**
PERFECT PAIRING PARTNER:	**Eat Real Lentil Chips Chilli & Lemon /prawn cocktail crisps**

With its light and effervescent taste, kombucha has become something of a phenomenon in recent years, helping to drive the growth and appreciation of no- and low-alcohol drinks. It's made by fermenting sweetened tea with specific strains of starter yeast, known as a scoby. Some plain styles retain more tea flavours, while some are distinctly sour. The most popular kombuchas are sweetened further and then flavoured with fruit juices, giving a wide versatility and flavour profile. As such, it's quite tricky to narrow down a specific pairing, but the lighter tea notes are easy to overpower with too much bold flavour, so look for complimentary elements: for instance, raspberry-flavoured kombucha sits very nicely with balsamic and sea salt crisps, lightly flavoured prawn cocktail crisps, as well as a lighter chilli flavour and citrus notes.

Why This Pairing Works

The more pronounced citrus elements in the chilli and lemon lentil chips really bring out the fresher, slightly tart raspberry notes nicely, and a touch of chilli brings some welcome heat. The sweetness in prawn cocktail crisps is also a real winner too!

Flavour Groups

Sweet/Fruity/Zesty/Heat

Which Brands To Try

No. 1 Living Raspberry & Pomegranate Kombucha, Left Field No. 2 Sencha Green Kombucha and Real Royal Flush Kombucha (all UK).

DRINKS GROUP:	**Non-alcoholic drinks**
TYPE:	**Tea and coffee**
PERFECT PAIRING PARTNER:	**Walkers Salt & Shake/Torres Fried Egg Crisps**

All those pairings have given me a hankering for something a little more down-to-earth... and what better beverage than a humble brew! A cup of builder's tea with a Hobnob biscuit is a pairing from the gods; however, in the name of science, pairing it with a packet of simple, ready salted crisps apparently has its benefits. According to a US professor of chemistry, Michelle Francl, adding a pinch of salt to your tea helps to counteract any bitter notes in an overbrewed mug. So, with the risk of starting a transatlantic cultural argument, let's give it a go! In addition, a morning cup of freshly brewed black Arabica coffee pairs nicely with some fried-egg-flavoured crisps... For the ultimate breakfast fry-up-style pairing, simply add in a bag of bacon Frazzles too.

Why This Pairing Works

The beauty of Salt & Shake crisps is you can season them to your particular taste and the science behind a little bit of salt with your brew (choose Yorkshire Tea, folks!) certainly works, bringing more of a natural herbal sweetness to the tea. Will it replace the Hobnob, though? Now there's a debate. As for the coffee and fried-egg crisps...

Well, I'll let you try this one for yourselves.

Flavour Groups

Earthy/Salty/Sweet/Malty

Which Brands To Try

I appreciate that everyone has their own preference when it comes to tea, so I won't be as silly as to tell you which one to pick... but definitely drink Yorkshire Tea!

DRINKS GROUP:	**Non-alcoholic drinks**
TYPE:	**Sparkling water**
PERFECT PAIRING PARTNER:	**Salt and vinegar crisps**

A seemingly difficult thing to pair, sparkling mineral water has a particularly good ability to clear the palate in-between tasting contrasting flavours, so when it comes to finding a perfect partner of its own, it's probably best to either play on this neutrality and go with something big, bold and flavoursome, or something simple and detailed, working with the natural saline/mineral notes in the water. Some brands on the market really play up to this and you'll even find 'water sommeliers' in upmarket restaurants these days, given the huge choice of styles and sources out there! Add a dash of fresh lime for a healthy lime and soda option, and seek out flavour-infused waters too.

Why This Pairing Works
The intensity of salt and vinegar crisps is especially heightened by the carbonation of the water and the palate really comes alive with the saline punch and acidic buzz of a well-made brand. A dash of fresh lime juice brings out a delicious fruity-citrus tang too.

Flavour Groups
Salty/Zesty/Earthy/Fruity

Which Brands To Try
Vichy Catalan (Spain), Dash Infused Sparkling Water (UK) and Perrier (France).

DRINKS GROUP:	**Non-alcoholic drinks**
TYPE:	**Lemonade**
PERFECT PAIRING PARTNER:	**Monster Munch Pickled Onion/ onion rings**

On a hot summer's day, if I've decided not to drink alcohol, there's nothing quite like a cold, refreshing glass of real, cloudy lemonade to see in an early-evening party or barbecue. That tangy bite, alongside the Mediterranean vibes emanating from the glass, transport me off to Sicily or another suitably exotic location. For a lemonade to work, it really needs that natural citric fruit flavour and for me, the sense that it's been made from nothing other than real lemons, sugar and sparkling water. When it comes to pairing, another big-hitting childhood classic works a treat: the familiar tang of Monster Munch Pickled Onion or a really decent onion ring.

Why This Pairing Works

Lemon and onion together really bring out the best in each other: the citrus notes bringing out the sweet and savoury tang in the onion and the slightly acidic pickled note bringing out the sweetness in the lemonade.

Flavour Groups

Zesty/Oniony/Sweet/Salty

Which Brands To Try

Fentimans Victorian Lemonade, Belvoir Freshly Squeezed Lemonade and R. Whites Traditional Cloudy Lemonade (all UK).

DRINKS GROUP:	**Non-alcoholic drinks**
TYPE:	**Dandelion and Burdock**
PERFECT PAIRING PARTNER:	**Smiths Frazzles Crispy Bacon/ bacon crisps**

From retro crisps to retro soft drinks! Dandelion and Burdock is the flavour of a generation: herbal and medicinal, it has a slightly fruity sweetness with spicy liquorice notes, making it not unlike a root beer. As a combination of flavours, it's certainly divisive, but one sip took me back to the time my parents used to have soft drinks delivered in reusable, two-litre glass bottles. I can think of only one worthy crisp that will truly do this justice – and what a pairing it is!

Why This Pairing Works

The sweet, salty and slightly smoky notes in the Frazzles really bring out the herbal flavours in the D&B, bringing a buttery texture in the mouth, alongside a huge smile. If ever there was a fond reminder of childhood summer holidays, it's this.

Flavour Groups

Herby/Earthy/Smoky/Meaty/Sweet

Which Brands To Try

Fentimans, Ben Shaws and Mr Fitzpatrick's Dandelion & Burdock Cordial (all UK).

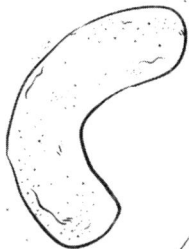

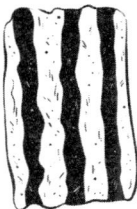

FESTIVE DRINKS

For wintery gatherings and new year's festivities!

DRINKS GROUP:	**Festive drinks**
TYPE:	**Mulled wine and cider**
PERFECT PAIRING PARTNER:	**Smoky bacon/roast turkey/pigs-in-blankets crisps/Stilton cheese straws**

For me, the festive season doesn't properly start until you smell the heady, spicy and welcoming aromas of mulled wine or cider wafting from the kitchen around the house. Historically a drink served in the winter markets across Eastern and Northern Europe, the UK has adopted it as the perfect festive tipple: it even gets a mention in Dickens' *A Christmas Carol*, where it is amusingly called the Smoking Bishop, ladled out from a large mitre-shaped punch bowl. For the best pairings think rich cheeses, spicy meat, smoky flavours and as a wild card, Stilton cheese straws.

Why This Pairing Works

Festive flavours like Stilton cheese bring saltiness and creaminess into the mix, alongside the rich fruitiness. Similarly, there's no better time to look out for festive limited-edition crisps, (think turkey and stuffing), which do all the pairing work for you! Some brands, such as Taylors Pigs in Blankets Crisps are available all year round, if, like me, you need a little festive pick-me-up before the season begins.

Flavour Groups

Salty/Cheesy/Fruity/Spicy/Meaty/Herby

The Perfect Mulled Recipe

There's a ton of great mulled wine recipes out there, but have you tried mulled cider? In a large pan, add three litres of quality dry cider (non-alcoholic cider or spicy apple juice will also work nicely), the rind from one lemon and orange, two teaspoons of cloves, two cinnamon sticks, one vanilla pod (split), one teaspoon of cardamon pods, three star anise and two teaspoons of pink peppercorns. Bring to the boil and then simmer for twelve minutes. Then add two tablespoons of muscovado sugar and 100 ml dark rum (optional). Simmer for a further ten minutes. Serve in warmed mugs.

DRINKS GROUP:	**Festive drinks**
TYPE:	**Snowball**
PERFECT PAIRING PARTNER:	**White-chocolate-coated pretzels**

The Snowball is a festive classic and arguably a hugely unappreciated cocktail, bringing sweetness, rich creaminess and a little zesty bite to the palate. At its heart is advocaat, the Dutch, custard-like liqueur made from eggs, cream and brandy: technically a boozy dessert in a bottle! Once the domain of your grandma's drinks cabinet, advocaat is a delight to use in festive cocktails and its smooth, silky thickness is more versatile than you think. The original Snowball recipe is quite bland: simply a mix of lemonade, lime juice and advocaat, but there's plenty you can do to pep up the complexity and make t a more refined, indulgent experience. When it comes to pairing, it's hard to escape the sweetness, so why not go along with it and bring in some chocolate too? To hell with the calories, IT'S CHRISTMAS!

Why This Pairing Works

The salty-sweet or 'swavoury' note here is great: a nice salty crunchiness from the pretzel, softened with the vanilla-heavy richness of the white chocolate. Throw in a few other flavours (see the recipe) and you can really elevate the cocktail and pairing to new heights.

Flavour Groups

Sweet/Creamy/Salty

The Perfect Snowball Recipe

In a large wine glass filled with ice, add 100 ml advocaat (classic Warninks), the juice of half a fresh lime, 25 ml oloroso sherry, 15 ml cherry liqueur and two dashes of chocolate bitters. Stir until well mixed. Top up with ginger ale, giving another quick stir to achieve a frothy head. Grate on some nutmeg and a little dark chocolate. Hey presto, a Snowball-sherry trifle in a cocktail!

PAIRINGS CHECKLIST

Red Wine

☐ Shiraz + M&S Thai Chilli Rice Crackers

☐ Merlot + Walkers or Lay's Roast Chicken

☐ Merlot + Simply Roasted Duck & Hoisin Crisps

☐ Pinot noir + Torres Black Truffle

☐ Pinot noir + Tyrrells Truffle & Sea Salt Crisps

☐ Malbec + McCoy's Flame-Grilled Steak Crisps

☐ Cabernet Sauvignon + Kettle Mature Cheddar & Red Onion Chips

☐ Cabernet Sauvignon + Burts Mature Cheddar & Onion Crisps

☐ Grenache + Walkers Sensations Regal Lamb & Mint

☐ Grenache + Kent Crisps Lamb & Rosemary

☐ Zinfandel/Primativo + Popchips Barbeque

☐ Zinfandel/Primativo + Lay's Barbecue Crisps

☐ Gamay + Torres Iberian Ham Crisps

☐ Tempranillo + Pipers Kirkby Malham Chorizo Crisps

☐ Sangiovese + Torres Mediterranean Herb Crisps

☐ Sangiovese + ParmCrisps Original Parmesan

White Wine

☐ Riesling + Native Sweet Chilli Pr*wn Crackers

☐ Riesling + Walkers Sensations Thai Sweet Chilli Crisps

☐ Pinot gris + Tyrrells Vegetable Crisps

☐ Pinot gris + Kettle Lightly Salted Veg Chips

☐ Pinot gris + Eat Real Tomato & Basil Hummus Chips

☐ Chardonnay + Brets Pesto Mozzarella

☐ Chardonnay + Tyrrells Pesto & Parmesan

- [ ] Chardonnay + M&S Honey Roast Ham Crisps
- [ ] Sauvignon blanc + Walkers Sensations Roast Chicken & Thyme or Regal Lamb & Mint
- [ ] Sauvignon blanc + Seabrook Lamb & Mint Crisps
- [ ] Picpoul + Kent Crisps Oyster & Vinegar
- [ ] Albariño/Alvarinho + Chipsticks Salt 'n' Vinegar Discos
- [ ] Albariño/Alvarinho + pickled onion crisps
- [ ] Moscato/Muscat + Lay's Cheese Flavoured Crisps
- [ ] Moscato/Muscat + Pringles Sour Cream & Onion
- [ ] Gewürztraminer + Walkers Sensations Lime & Coriander Chutney Poppadoms
- [ ] Gewürztraminer + Simply Roasted Duck & Hoisin Crisps
- [ ] Viognier + McCoy's Thai Sweet Chicken Crisps
- [ ] Viognier + Nik Naks Rib 'n' Saucy
- [ ] Viognier + Herr's Baby Back Ribs Chips
- [ ] Chenin blanc + Jacob's Cracker Crisps Sour Cream & Chive
- [ ] Rosé wine + Burts Firecracker Lobster Crisps
- [ ] Rosé wine + Proper Prawn Cocktail Chips
- [ ] Rosé wine + Salty Dog Barbecue Rib Crisps
- [ ] Orange wine + Tyrrells Vegetable Crisps

Sparkling Wine

- [ ] Champagne + Walkers Classic Ready Salted
- [ ] Champagne + McCoy's Ready Salted
- [ ] Champagne + Piper's Anglesey Sea Salt Crisps
- [ ] Prosecco + Tyrrells Vegetable or Sweet Chilli & Red Pepper
- [ ] Prosecco + M&S Prosciutto & Formaggio Crisps
- [ ] Cava + Ten Acre Fried Chicken
- [ ] Cava + Real Hand Cooked Chicken Peri-Peri Crisps
- [ ] Rosé + Prawn Cocktail Skips
- [ ] Rosé + Lister's Prawn Cocktail
- [ ] Rosé + Tatyo Prawn Cocktail Crisps

Sweet Wine

☐ Sauternes + Kettle Mature Cheddar & Red Onion Chips

☐ Sauternes + Taste of Game Wild Duck

☐ Sauternes + Wild Boar Crisps

☐ Tokaji + Bret Blue Cheese & Pancetta

☐ Tokaji + Burts Smoked Crispy Bacon Crisps

Fortified Wine

☐ Sherry + Manomasa Manchego & Green Olive Tortilla Chips

☐ Sherry + Pipers Kirkby Malham Chorizo

☐ Sherry + Torres Black Truffle Crisps

☐ Port (ruby and tawny) + Kettle Mature Cheddar & Red Onion Chips

☐ Port (ruby and tawny) + Simply Roasted Duck & Hoisin Crisps

☐ Port (ruby and tawny) + Proper Barbecue Lentil Chips

☐ Port (white) + Tyrrells Pesto & Parmesan Crisps

☐ Port (white) + Made For Drink Chorizo Thins

☐ Port (white) + Serious Pig Crunchy Snacking Cheese

Light Beer

☐ IPA + Kent Crisps Oyster & Vinegar

☐ IPA + Burts Sea Salt & Malt Vinegar Crisps

☐ Pilsner + Real Handcooked Ham & English Mustard

☐ Pilsner + Salty Dog Ham & Mustard

☐ Pilsner + Two Farmers Hereford Hop Cheese & Onion Crisps

☐ Wheat beer + Walkers Wotsits Cheese

☐ Wheat beer + Walkers Quavers Cheese

☐ Wheat beer + crunchy banana chips

☐ Lager + Walkers Salt & Vinegar Crisps

☐ Lager + prawn crackers

☐ Lager + Poppadoms Originals

☐ Saison + Walkers Roast Chicken

☐ Saison + Sensations Roast Chicken & Thyme Crisps

☐ Blonde + Walkers Max Punchy Paprika

- ☐ Blonde + Tyrrells Smoked Paprika Crisps
- ☐ Sour + Torres Cured Cheese Crisps
- ☐ Sour + Howdah Masala Dippers

Dark Beer

- ☐ Bitter Ale + Pipers Great Berwick Longhorn Beef
- ☐ Bitter Ale + McCoy's Flame-Grilled Steak
- ☐ Bitter Ale + Sussex Crisp Co. Rib of Sussex Beef with Horseradish Crisps
- ☐ Stout and Porter + bacon fries
- ☐ Stout and Porter + smoky bacon crisps
- ☐ Red ale + Popchips Barbeque
- ☐ Red ale + Pringles Texas BBQ Sauce
- ☐ Brown ale + Doritos Tangy Cheese
- ☐ Lambic fruit beer + Cheetos Twisted Sweet & Spicy or Flamin' Hot
- ☐ Lambic fruit beer + black peppercorn and salt crisps
- ☐ Rauchbier + Yorkshire Crisps Sweet Cured Ham & Pickle
- ☐ Rauchbier + Torres Black Truffle Crisps
- ☐ Rauchbier + Mr Trotter's English Mustard Pork Crackling

Cider

- ☐ Dry/cask-aged vintage cider + Mr Trotter's Pork Crackling
- ☐ Dry/cask-aged vintage cider + Beerpig Pork Crackling
- ☐ Dry/cask-aged vintage cider + Perfectly Vegan Lentil Crackling Smoky Bacon
- ☐ Sweet cider + Walkers BBQ Pork Ribs Crisps
- ☐ Sweet cider + vegetable crisps
- ☐ Fruit cider + smoky bacon
- ☐ Fruit cider + sea salt and balsamic vinegar
- ☐ Fruit cider + black pepper crisps

Gin Cocktails

- ☐ Negroni + Jacob's Cracker Crisps Sea Salt & Balsamic Vinegar
- ☐ Negroni + Kettle Sea Salt & Balsamic Chips
- ☐ Gibson + Monster Munch Pickled Onion

- ☐ Gibson + Space Raiders Pickled Onion
- ☐ Gin & Tonic + Asda Extra Special Sea Salt & Chardonnay Wine Vinegar Crisps
- ☐ Classic Gin Martini + Tyrrells Mediterranean Herb
- ☐ Classic Gin Martini + Brindisa Patatas Sarriegui
- ☐ Classic Gin Martini + Manomasa Manchego & Green Olive Tortilla Chips

Tequila and Mezcal Cocktails

- ☐ Paloma + Walkers Max Strong Jalapeño & Cheese
- ☐ Paloma + Real Handcooked Jalapeño Pepper Crisps
- ☐ Margarita + Takis Fuego Hot Chilli Pepper & Lime Corn Snacks
- ☐ Bloody Maria + Doritos Chilli Heatwave
- ☐ Bloody Maria + Manomasa Serrano Chilli & Yucatan Honey Tortilla Chips
- ☐ Mezcal Old Fashioned + Salted roasted pecan nuts
- ☐ Mezcal Old Fashioned + Smiths Bacon Fries
- ☐ Mezcal Old Fashioned + Smiths Frazzles Crispy Bacon

Whisk(e)y Cocktails

- ☐ Highball + Kettle Sea Salt & Crushed Black Peppercorn Chips
- ☐ Highball + Smiths Scampi Fries
- ☐ Highball + Proper Barbecue Lentil Chips
- ☐ Penicillin + Walkers Sensations Thai Sweet Chilli
- ☐ Penicillin + Tyrrells Sweet Chilli & Red Pepper Crisps
- ☐ Irish Whiskey & Cola + Tayto Smoky Bacon Crisps
- ☐ Old Fashioned + Lay's Barbecue Chips
- ☐ Old Fashioned + Popchips Barbeque
- ☐ Manhattan + Sea salt and balsamic vinegar crisps

Vodka Cocktails

- ☐ Bloody Mary + Twiglets
- ☐ Bloody Mary + Pringles Sour Cream & Onion
- ☐ Bloody Mary + Seabrook Worcestershire Sauce Crisps

☐ Espresso Martini + Parm Crisps Original Parmesan

☐ Espresso Martini + Whisps Parmesan Crisps

☐ Espresso Martini + M&S Cheese Straws

☐ Cosmopolitan + Manomesa Green Lemon & Pink Peppercorn Tortilla Chips

☐ Cosmopolitan + Walkers Sensations Crushed Sea Salt & Black Peppercorn Crisps

☐ Porn Star Martini + Tyrrells Posh Prawn Cocktail Crisps

☐ Porn Star Martini + Prawn Cocktail Skips

Rum Cocktails

☐ Daiquiri + Yorkshire Crisps Sweet Chilli & Lime

☐ Daiquiri + The Dormen Sweet Chilli & Lime Crisps

☐ Mojito + McCoy's Thai Sweet Chicken

☐ Mojito + Pipers Wild Thyme & Rosemary Crisps

Other Cocktails

☐ Aperol Spritz + M&S Italian Style Pancetta Crisps

☐ Aperol Spritz + Brindisa Patatas Sarriegui

☐ Aperol Spritz + Torres Extra Virgin Olive Oil

☐ Aperol Spritz + balsamic vinegar and sea salt crisps

☐ Brandy Sparkler + Torres Black Truffle

☐ Brandy Sparkler + Tyrrel s Truffle & Sea Salt Crisps

Interesting World Drinks

☐ Saké + Kettle Asian Chil i Beef Chips

☐ Saké + Monster Munch Sweet & Spicy Flamin' Hot

☐ Aquavit + Pipers Jalapeño & Dill Crisps

☐ Aquavit + Estrella Dill Chips

☐ Aquavit + Oh My Hog! Salt & Vinegar Pork Crunch

☐ Pisco + Walkers Sensations Roasted Chicken & Thyme

☐ Pisco + Char-grilled Chimichurri Crisps

☐ Pisco + McCoy's Sizzling King Prawn Crisps

☐ Shochu and Soju + Koikeya Wasabi Nori

☐ Shochu and Soju + Tesco Roast Beef & Horseradish Crisps

Non-alcoholic Drinks

☐ Ginger Beer + Walkers Sensations Lime & Coriander Chutney Poppadoms

☐ Orangina + Lay's 3D Bacon Bugles

☐ Orangina + Walkers Southern Style BBQ Bugles

☐ Kombucha + Eat Real Lentil Chips Chilli & Lemon

☐ Kombucha + prawn cocktail crisps

☐ Tea and coffee + Walkers Salt & Shake

☐ Tea and coffee + Torres Fried Egg Crisps

☐ Sparkling water + Salt and vinegar crisps

☐ Lemonade + Monster Munch Pickled Onion

☐ Lemonade + onion rings

☐ Dandelion and Burdock + Smiths Frazzles Crispy Bacon

☐ Dandelion and Burdock + bacon crisps

Festive Drinks

☐ Ginger Beer + Walkers Sensations Lime & Coriander Chutney Poppadoms

☐ Mulled wine and cider + smoky bacon

☐ Mulled wine and cider + roast turkey

☐ Mulled wine and cider + pigs-in-blankets crisps

☐ Mulled wine and cider + Stilton cheese straws

☐ Snowball + white-chocolate-coated pretzels

INDEX OF
FLAVOURS

Index

Wheat beer 74

Meaty
Aperol Spritz 126
Aquavit 131
Bitter ale 82
Bloody Mary 116
Cava 58
Chardonnay 44
Dandelion and Burdock 142
Gamay 37
Grenache 35
Irish whiskey & cola 110
Malbec 33
Merlot 31
Mezcal Old Fashioned 105
Mulled wine and cider 146
Old Fashioned 111
Orange wine 53
Pilsner 73
Pisco 132
Port – ruby and tawny 67
Rauchbier 87
Red ale 84
Rosé wine 52
Saison beer 76
Sauternes 62
Sauvignon blanc 45
Sherry 66
Stout and porter 83
Sweet cider 91
Tempranillo 38
Tokaji 63
Vintage cider 90
Zinfandel/Primativo 36

Nutty
Bitter ale 82
Brown ale 85
Gin Martini 99

Mezcal Old Fashioned 105
Port – ruby and tawny 67
Red ale 84
Sauternes 62
Sherry 66

Oniony
Albariño/Alvarinho 47
Bitter ale 82
Bloody Mary 116
Cabernet Sauvignon 34
Chenin blanc 51
Gibson 97
Lemonade 141
Malbec 33

Salty
Albariño/Alvarinho 47
Aperol Spritz 126
Bitter ale 82
Champagne 56
Espresso Martini 117
Gamay 37
Gin and tonic 98
Grenache 35
Highball 108
IPA beer 72
Lager 75
Lemonade 141
Manhattan 112
Mezcal Old Fashioned 105
Mulled wine and cider 146
Negroni 96
Orange wine 53
Picpoul 46
Pinot gris 43
Port – white 68
Prosecco 57
Sangiovese 39
Sherry 66

Index

Index